For our elders and ancestors,
whose voices were silenced but
whose courage created us.

ACKNOWLEDGMENTS

This edition of The Virginia Indian Heritage Trail was made possible by funds from the Virginia Tourism Corporation and the Virginia Council on Indians. The first edition was funded by grants from the following agencies: Jamestown 2007, the Virginia Department of Historic Resources, the Virginia Tourism Corporation, the Virginia General Assembly, and the Virginia Foundation for the Humanities. We thank the Virginia Indian tribal leaders for planning assistance and insight as the project progressed, and those tribal members who developed the tribal history pages included here. Thanks also to the members of the Virginia Council on Indians for their help in envisioning this project during its early years.

Special thanks to Robert Llewellyn for photographic images used throughout this booklet, a number of which were first published in *Empires in the Forest* (2006) by Avery Chenowith (text) and Robert Llewellyn (photography), University of Virginia Press, with partial funding from the Virginia Foundation for the Humanities. To David Bearinger, Virginia Foundation for the Humanities, for assistance with development and review and for thoughtful advice at difficult times. To Keith Damiani, Sequoia Design, and Mathias Tornqvist, design photographer.

Thanks also to Deanna Beacham, Program Specialist, Virginia Council on Indians, for contributing biographical vignettes, text review, and early supervision of this project. To Robert Chris French, Rhyannon Berkowitz, and Buck Woodard, Heritage Trail reviewers, for insightful analysis of interpretive sites throughout the state. To staff members of those sites for their assistance.

To the members of the Virginia Indian Nations Summit on Higher Education for inspiration over the years. To Betsy Barton, Virginia Department of Education, for enthusiastic support.

The Virginia Foundation for the Humanities
145 Ednam Drive
Charlottesville, Virginia 22903
(434) 924-3296 phone
(434) 296-4714 fax
www.virginiafoundation.org

As you explore the Virginia Indian cultures and the sites in this book, take advantage of the unique lodging, restaurants and other attractions along the way. For more information about traveling in Virginia, visit *www.virginia.org*

CONTENTS

FOREWORD

by CHIEF KENNETH F. ADAMS (UPPER MATTAPONI)

As Americans, we are taught to respect our heritage. As American Indians, our heritage spans more than 10,000 years. Yet, in the Commonwealth of Virginia, there has been a meager respect for the contributions of such a lengthy history. To the average Virginian, Virginia Indian history began in 1607 and ended in 1700. A 10,000 year history has been compressed into fewer than 100 years.

There is so much more to the Virginia Indian story. The Heritage Trail will help immensely in filling this historic void. As a people we were respectful to our environment, living in harmony with the land and our Creator in several hundred vibrant communities in this land some called *Tsenacomoco*. In those communities were places of worship, places of recreation, and land set aside for agriculture. There were large houses fit for kings and smaller houses where several families lived. Even so, most Americans have read we were savages, and we have been portrayed throughout history as a people to be conquered and tossed aside.

We have an opportunity with this Trail to portray the Virginia Indian in a proper light. Our heritage is due respect as well as any other heritage. Our history needs to be told as well as any other history. We cannot continue to be the forgotten people in the Virginia history books or on the landmarks across this Commonwealth. Our Creator placed us here as the gatekeepers of this land, and our magnificent story cannot and will not be buried.

A PLACE FOR THE NATIVE VOICE

by **RHYANNON BERKOWITZ (CREEK)**
Graduate Student, Department of Anthropology, University of Virginia

In 1607, the first permanent English settlement in North America was founded on a small island that came to be known as Jamestown. Combined with Spanish forces in the Florida territory and French colonialists in Canada, the British occupation of Virginia had a devastating impact on the indigenous peoples of this land. This came not just in the form of physical and overt violence; often it was much more subtle. Perhaps most appalling was the attempt to simply write American Indians out of existence.

Whether it was through colonial disenfranchisement edicts, scholarly writings that convinced adherents of the inevitable disappearance of Virginia's Native people, the passage of laws such as the 1924 Act to Preserve Racial Integrity, or policies which attempted to erase Indian identity, the effect has been to exclude Virginia Indians from history and confine them to the distant past.

Yet they have not disappeared. In fact, Virginia Indians have survived and flourished; today, the eight recognized tribes

> Native peoples recognize not only the connection between the past, present, and future, but also **the innate connection we have to each other as people.**

in the Commonwealth are strong political and cultural forces. Perhaps most importantly, Virginia Indians are now finally being allowed—even asked—to tell their own stories.

The importance of including Native voices in the presentation of Virginia history cannot be overstated. No longer will Virginia's Native peoples be viewed as disembodied objects relegated to the past; now, they will be seen as living peoples with vibrant and thriving cultures. Their voices will enrich the history of this state, allowing citizens and visitors alike to gain a deeper understanding of past historical occurrences, both good and bad, that have brought us to the present and that will continue to affect us well into the future.

Native peoples recognize not only the connection between the past, present, and future, but also the innate connection we have to each other as people. While Virginia Indian stories relate experiences that were lived by tribal members, that history is not exclusive; for better or for worse, the history of Virginia Indians is our history. As more stories are told, as more of our shared history is learned, we will begin to create an understanding of who we are today, not only as Virginians and Americans, but as human beings.

ARCHAEOLOGY AND VIRGINIA INDIAN HISTORY

by **JEFFREY L. HANTMAN, PH.D.**
Associate Professor, Department of Anthropology
Director, Interdisciplinary Program in Archaeology
University of Virginia

Archaeology of American Indian sites in Virginia is almost always done today in collaboration with Virginia's Indian nations and the Virginia Council on Indians, in contrast to the way it was usually done in the past. More and more archaeologists are learning that artifacts and sites are not impersonal scientific objects but are part of the lives of the ancestors of Virginia's first people, as well as their descendants. Collaborative archaeology provides an alternative voice in the writing of Virginia's Indian history. This voice is one that fills the long silences spanning the millennia before Europeans arrived, as well as the critical silences that exist within colonial-era documents. A brief review of some archaeological sites illustrates how archaeology helps to fill in the silences of history to offer new perspectives on Virginia's past.

We can start at what some might call the beginning, if there is such a moment. Cactus Hill, on the Nottoway River in southeast Virginia, is an archaeological site that challenges a long-held orthodoxy that Indian peo-

ple throughout America first entered the continent from the west at 10,000 BC, crossing over the Bering Land Bridge into Alaska. Many Native people have challenged this model, based on their religious beliefs and oral histories regarding migrations.

The artifacts at the site are 5,000 years older than the Bering Land Bridge theory would allow. Along with several other contemporaneous sites in the

Eastern U.S., Cactus Hill opens new questions about where the first Indian people came from, if they did arrive from someplace else; about how they arrived (by boat?); and lends a voice to those who would push the history of Virginia's first people into a much deeper, if not timeless, past.

Archaeological sites in Virginia also confront a long-held and unfounded stereotype that portrayed Indians as part of nature, adapting passively to, rather than actually creating, the ecosystem of which they were a part. English colonists wrote that the Virginia environment they encountered in the seventeenth century was a primeval (undisturbed) forest. This was a powerful and self-serving myth, because the English believed unimproved land was not owned and therefore open for the taking. They did not recognize the improvements and investments that had already been made in the land they took.

Archaeological sites bear testimony to how Virginia Indians culturally transformed their environment. They burned the forest systematically to increase productivity for both hunting and gathering. They enhanced the growth of local native starchy plants which became food staples, such as *chenopodium* (goosefoot). They successfully adopted non-local plants such as squash, corn and beans to their soils and into their diets. And, they maintained population levels in balance with their changing economies. Cultures of dynamic sustainability and choice, rather than passivity and dependence, can be read in the thousands of American Indian sites dotting the Virginia landscape in the many millennia following the first known settlements.

In the centuries just before the English arrived, surplus agricultural production, population growth, and the development of social hierarchies all became part of Virginia Indian society. It is a question as to how and why those changes came about. In the Virginia Algonquian world of the coastal plain, this hierarchical society has often been viewed as the rapid centralization of power by one man--known to the English as the paramount chief Powhatan. Native beliefs and ethnography question the idea that one individual in Indian society would have such unchecked authority. Native experts note, for instance, that priests provided a critical check and balance of power in those times. Archaeological study of Werowocomoco, Powhatan's town at the time of European arrival, has provided some new perspectives.

Studies at Werowocomoco uncovered a landscape marked by the distinctive construction of seven hundred feet of ditches, which divided the town into separate spheres. These ditches were culturally meaningful markers demarcating the power of and within the place. Significantly, the ditches were first built in the thirteenth century. The archaeological evidence suggests that Powhatan moved to Werowocomoco not to create a seat of authority, but more likely to inhabit an already consecrated place of power.

Colonial observations were particularly skewed in their descriptions of Indian people with whom they had little interaction—such as the Monacan of the Virginia interior. Based on second-hand information, the Monacan were portrayed as few in number, dispersed, non-agricultural, and hostile. But, archaeological surveys in the interior show this region to have been densely occupied, and the ancient towns yield evidence of maize and squash agriculture. Most importantly, the Piedmont and Blue Ridge regions of Virginia were marked by the presence of earthen burial mounds, unlike any others found in Virginia. These mounds are the heart of the Monacan homeland. They are sacred places in which the bones of the ancestors were ritually buried in ceremonies that took place periodically *over centuries*, building the mound higher and higher over time.

In 1784, Thomas Jefferson transformed one of these mounds into the first scientifically studied archaeological site in North America. Jefferson was interested in how and why the mounds were constructed, and he used archaeological methods to make sense of this place in his own terms. However, it was not an archaeological site to the Monacan people whom Jefferson observed performing mournful ceremonies there in the 1750s. And it was not an archaeological site to the Monacan people who returned again to this place in 2001 and conducted a blessing ritual. To these Monacan tribal members, past and present, the mound remains first a place of and for the ancestors. No further excavations will take place there, and human remains from nearby mound sites, long held in museums, have been returned to the Monacan people for reburial, with the help of archaeologists. These mounds, like all Virginia Indian archaeological sites, must be given the respect due to the ancestors, and spoken for by their descendants. Only then, working collaboratively and respectfully, can archaeology fulfill its formidable challenge to help fill in the silences that for too long have shaped and distorted so much of Virginia's Indian history.

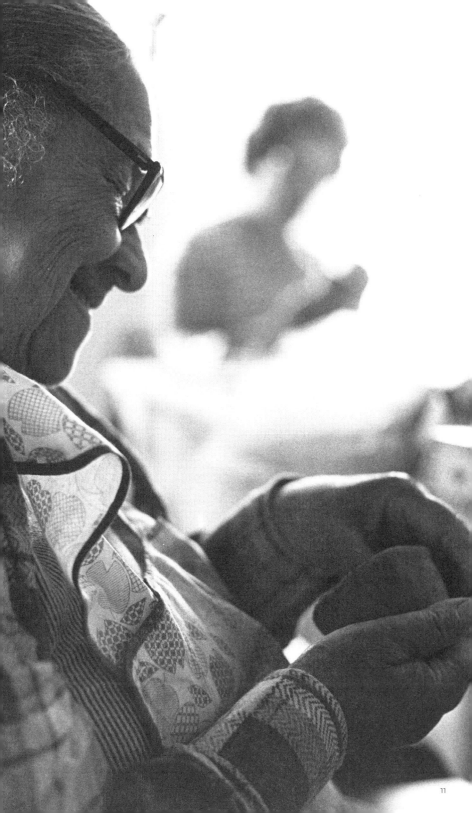

VIRGINIA INDIANS: OUR STORY

by **KARENNE WOOD (MONACAN)**
Director, Virginia Indian Heritage Program

Native peoples have lived in the area we now call Virginia for as many as 17,000 years, according to archeologists. However, if you ask Virginia Indians how long our people have been here, they will probably say, "We have always been here." Our histories, our ancestral connections, and our traditions are intertwined with the land called *Tsenacomoco* by Virginia Algonquian peoples. It is a bountiful land, given to us by the Creator as the place most fitting for us to live.

The early inhabitants of Virginia were hunter-gatherers who followed migratory patterns of animals, but over time, they settled into specific areas, usually along the riverbanks, and outlined their territories. Our people developed intimate, balanced relationships with the animals, plants, and geographic formations that characterized our homelands. History books seldom refer to the sophisticated agricultural techniques we practiced for more than 900 years or to the managed landscapes we developed, where hunting and fishing areas alternated with townships and croplands arranged along the waterways. They seldom note that Native nutrition was far superior to what was available in Europe before the colonial era, or that our knowledge of astron-

CELEBRATION OR COMMEMORATION?

The founding of the Jamestown Colony in May 1607 marked the first successful settlement of the English on this continent. It was not the beginning of democracy or of free enterprise, both of which existed among some indigenous tribes before Europeans arrived. It began a developmental process that created the United States of America and, much later, equal opportunity. It also began the processes of American Indian marginalization, racism, and environmental depredation that followed.

For Virginia Indians, the quadricentennial is a time to reflect on our ancestors' sacrifices and our survival, an opportunity to examine our collective past and to plan for the future of unborn generations. It is a time for honest assessment. Would Powhatan or John Smith be pleased to see what Virginia has become? How can we ensure that during the next 400 years we will honor the contributions of all our communities and protect the environmental gifts that surround us?

omy informed our farming calendars as well as navigation by night. Native peoples developed complex social and religious systems as well as vast trade networks that extended thousands of miles. Monacan people built impressive burial mounds throughout their homeland, and the Powhatan developed a complicated tributary system that influenced political and social relationships. Virginia was not a wilderness to us; it was a known and loved home place, and we shared our resources with strangers as well as within our communities. That is the Native way.

The English were not the first Europeans to visit the Chesapeake Bay region. Spanish ships began exploring its waterways during the early 1500s and occasionally captured Native boys. The "lost colony" of Roanoke was established by the English in the 1580s but failed within a few years. An English ship was attacked by Indians on the Bay in 1603, and the ship's captain was killed. Sometime shortly

thereafter, European sailors—most likely English—were welcomed by the Rappahannock chief, whom they killed. They then took several Indian prisoners and left. These may have been the same Indian men who were seen demonstrating dugout canoes on the Thames River in England.

When the English colonists arrived in our homeland in the spring of 1607, perhaps 20,000 Algonquian-speaking peoples were incorporated into several paramount chiefdoms such as the Powhatan and Patawomeke, or into independent tribes such as the Chickahominy and Rappahannock. A similar number of Siouan-speaking people were located to the west, in the piedmont and mountain regions of Virginia, members of a loosely confederated alliance that included the Monacan, Mannahoac, Saponi, Nahyssan, Occaneechi, and Tutelo (Totero) tribes. There were also Iroquoian-speaking Cherokee in the southwestern area, as well as the Nottoway and Meherrin tribes south of

NATIVE LANGUAGES AND CORRESPONDING VIRGINIA TRIBES

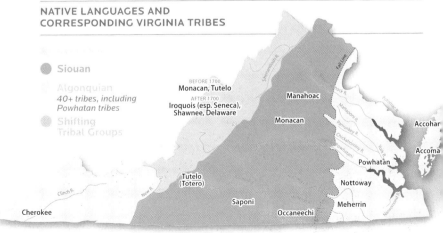

Siouan

Algonquian
40+ tribes, including
Powhatan tribes

Shifting
Tribal Groups

BEFORE 1700
Monacan, Tutelo

AFTER 1700
Iroquois (esp. Seneca),
Shawnee, Delaware

Manahoac

Monacan

Accohar

Accoma

Powhatan

Tutelo
(Totero)

Nottoway

Cherokee

Saponi

Occaneechi

Meherrin

Powhatan's domain. Within a century, the Algonquian tribes were reduced to just several hundred individuals. Similar depopulations occurred among other indigenous peoples throughout the East coast and inland regions as European settlements spread westward. Through disease and then warfare, Native peoples of this continent were decimated, and their lands were taken from them. It has been estimated that, in some areas, as much as ninety percent of the Native population succumbed to European diseases such as smallpox, to which the people had developed no immunity.

Initially, the settlers were welcomed, first by the Kecoughtan at the mouth of the Chesapeake Bay, and then by the Paspahegh, who became the closest neighbors to Jamestown. Relations deteriorated quickly, however, due to cultural misunderstandings and deceptions on both sides. Indian raids on the English started within a short time of their arrival, and from then on, relations alternated between uneasy truces and outright hostilities. Meanwhile, the starving English attempted to trade for corn with several tribes, and when they were refused, they took it by force. The first real English war

WHO WAS POWHATAN?

When the English arrived in Virginia in 1607, Powhatan, whose informal name was Wahunsunacock, was the acknowledged paramount chief, or *mamanatowick*, of more than 32 tribes, with more than 150 towns. These tribes ranged from the Potomac River in the north to just south of the James River in the south, and from the fall line of the rivers in the west to the Atlantic Ocean.

Powhatan, who was probably in his 60s when he first met the English, had acquired leadership of these tribes through inheritance and coercion that was frequently reinforced with family or marriage ties. He held his position not only through military strength but also through great personal and spiritual charisma as well as a complex system of social rules not fully understood by the English. The tribes under Powhatan's leadership paid tribute to his treasury in food and goods, which were then used for redistribution, trade, rewards, and ceremonial display.

In the early years of the English colony, Powhatan's first intent was probably to incorporate the English into his polity as another tribe. Thwarted by the English, who had another agenda, he retired from leadership around 1616 and died in April 1618.

with Virginia Algonquian tribes began in 1610, when Lord de la Warr ordered attacks on the Kecoughtan and the Paspahegh, and the English soldiers brutally killed Indian women and children as well as the fighting men. This was a shock to the Virginia Indian peoples, who did not kill women and children during warfare but incorporated them into the tribe that prevailed. After Pocahontas was captured by the English in 1613, and then through her marriage to John Rolfe and subsequent visit to England, several years of peace occurred.

WHO WAS OPECHANCANOUGH?

Opechancanough, a leading chief or *werowance* of the Pamunkey nation, was a maternal relative of the paramount chief Powhatan. Identified as one of Powhatan's successors to the paramount chiefdom, he also acted as war chief or military leader for Powhatan. Opechancanough was leading the party of Indians who captured Captain John Smith when Smith went on an exploratory venture up the Chickahominy River late in 1607.

It was Opechancanough who organized the attacks against the English colonists living outside of Jamestown in 1622, in an attempt to punish them for encroaching on lands that Powhatan had not granted them. The English interpreted these attacks as an attempt to oust them from Virginia, and they retaliated with hostilities against the Indians for several years.

After Opechancanough became paramount chief in 1629, he organized similar attacks in 1644. He was unable to walk and was carried on a hurdle to the ensuing skirmishes. Shortly thereafter, when he was nearly 100 years old, he was captured by the English and imprisoned at Jamestown, where he was killed when a prison guard shot him in the back. Opechancanough is still revered today by Virginia Indians as a hero and early protector of our lands.

Pocahontas died in England in 1617, and Powhatan died the following year. Within a few short years, the colony was at war again. During the first Great Attack, led by Opechancanough in 1622, about one third of the English were killed. The second attack, in 1644, was followed by the capture and murder of Opechancanough. The Treaty of 1646 established English dominion over the Lower Peninsula and the requirement that Indian tribes pay tribute to the Governor of Virginia, a practice that continues today among the Pamunkey and Mattaponi tribes in the form of the Annual Treaty Tribute ceremony, which is held at the Governor's Mansion on the day before Thanksgiving.

In 1676, Nathaniel Bacon sparked a rebellion against Governor Berkeley, during which he raided the friendly Pamunkey, killing many of the people. Bacon attacked other Virginia Algonquian tribes as well. He also betrayed his Occaneechi allies, a branch of the Siouan confederation to the west, killing most of them after they had helped him to defeat a Susquehannock group. The 1677 Treaty that followed, signed by the powerful Pamunkey *werowansqua* Cockacoeske and other Indian leaders, established the signatory tribes as subjects of the King of England and required that they hold their lands by patent of the Crown. No English were to settle within three miles of an Indian town, a law that was subsequently violated innumerable times. The travel and trade of Indian nations was heavily regulated.

In 1691, the Brafferton School at the College of William and Mary began to educate young Indian men. Another Indian school, primarily for Saponi youth, was established at Fort Christanna in 1714. Fort Christanna served as a center for trade between the colony and tribes located farther south and as an important security buffer for the colonial settlements. After the Fort closed, some Saponi students attended the Brafferton School. This practice of educating Indian children as an assimilation attempt was later bureaucratized by the United States into the boarding schools where Indian children from throughout the country were sent. One of these schools served African-Americans and Indians separately; it was located in Hampton, Virginia.

Throughout the 18th and 19th centuries, Virginia Indian people found themselves policed by the colonial government, reduced to poverty as their landholdings eroded or were stolen outright. The Tutelo, a branch of the Monacan confederacy, left the area to ally with the Iroquois to the north, and a number of other tribes moved out of Virginia and other neighboring states. The remaining Indians' cultures changed slowly over the years; tribal members adopted European tools and farming techniques, hunted for the deerskin and fur trade as well as subsistence, and were introduced to Christianity and early American customs.

Virginia Indians have defended their homelands in every war in which the U.S. has engaged. Tribal members fought in the Revolutionary and Civil Wars, sometimes on opposing sides, and some emerged as early activists during these difficult times. The Upper

Mattaponi and Monacan tribes have maintained oral histories of several Revolutionary War veterans. In 1829, the South Carolina court of appeals rejected the appeal of a Pamunkey Indian, a veteran of the Continental Army, who received a federal pension and had petitioned for the right to vote.

During the Civil War, a number of Pamunkey men chose to serve the Union Army as pilots, in an effort to protect their community from Virginia authorities who had repeatedly attempted to disarm and dispossess them of their reservation. These men were thrown off the rolls of the Colosse Baptist church for serving the Yankees. The group included Terrill Bradby, who went on to become a Union spy and gunboat pilot, and who received a pension for his war service. Bradby later worked with anthropologists James Mooney and Albert Gatschet, teaching them about Powhatan culture, and he

WHO WAS POCAHONTAS?

Pocahontas, a daughter of the paramount chief Powhatan, was about 10 years old in 1607, when the captive John Smith was brought to her father's headquarters at Werowocomoco. She was noted for being bright and curious. Opinions differ as to whether the famous "rescue of John Smith" incident actually happened, but if it did, it was most likely a form of ritual misunderstood by Smith. During the next two years, Pocahontas sometimes accompanied her father's councilors on trips to Jamestown.

In 1613, while she was visiting with the Patawomeke people in what is now Stafford County, the teenager was kidnapped by the English and held for ransom. During her captivity, Pocahontas met the Englishman John Rolfe, who wanted to marry her. After the English made peace with her father, she agreed, with her father's approval, to accept their religion and marry Rolfe. She took the name Rebecca. The peace that followed lasted for several years, during which the English steadily added to their land holdings from her people's territory.

In 1616, the Rolfes went to England with their young son Thomas, where Rebecca Rolfe was presented to the English court. She died there of an unknown disease in 1617, and she was buried in Gravesend. In 2006, a delegation of Virginia Indians visited her grave and honored her as one of our ancestors who faced difficult decisions and did her best for her people.

was sent to represent his people at the Columbian Exposition of the World's Fair in Chicago in 1893.

In Virginia Indian history, the first half of the 20th century is dominated by issues resulting from state-sanctioned racial policies. The first Race Laws were passed in Virginia in 1705; more followed in 1866, and the Racial Integrity Act passed in 1924. It prohibited marriage to whites by people of color, including Indians. In 1967 the U.S. Supreme Court overturned it as unconstitutional. In 1912, Dr. Walter Plecker became the state registrar of the Bureau of Vital Statistics in Richmond and remained in his position until 1946. He was a staunch advocate for eugenics, the pseudo-science of race. Plecker believed that there should be only two races of people in Virginia, white and "colored," that white people were superior, and that people of "mixed" race would produce defective children. By 1925 he had decided, based mainly on conjecture, that there were no "pure" Indians in Virginia. He developed a list of surnames, people he believed to be "mixed," and he sent instructions to local clerks of courts, hospital personnel, school administrators and others, informing them that persons with these names were not to associate with white people. He altered numerous birth certificates of Indian people, noting their race as "colored." Plecker was challenged in court during the 1940s by two Monacan men, Roy and Winston Branham, who had been classified as colored for the draft, and by other Monacan people who questioned his right to change their birth certificates. Ultimately, he was forced to admit that no evidence supported his actions.

Most of the current tribes in Virginia established churches and sometimes mission schools during the early years of the 20th century, and many of the people accepted Christianity. The schools provided up to a seventh-grade education for those children who were able to attend. Indians were not allowed to attend white schools, and they refused to attend black schools. Many Indian children were needed to

WHO WAS AMOROLECK?

While exploring the upper reaches of the Rappahannock River in 1608, near present-day Fredericksburg, John Smith and his men encountered a group of warriors who fired arrows at them from the shoreline and then disappeared into the woods. Smith decided to investigate and encountered a wounded man who had been left behind. Smith's Powhatan guide attempted to kill the man, declaring him to be an enemy, but Smith intervened and spoke with him through a translator.

The wounded man identified himself as Amoroleck, a member of the Mannahoac alliance of Siouan-speaking tribes, who were hunting in the region. When asked about the worlds he knew, he described the Powhatan world, then his own, and a third nation of Indians who lived to the northwest—possibly the Haudenosaunee, later called Iroquois by Europeans. Smith asked why the Mannahoac people had reacted with hostility when he was coming in friendship. Amoroleck replied, "We heard that you were a people come from the underworld, to take our world from us."

Amoroleck conducted Smith and his men to his people's hunting camp, where they were welcomed with a feast and dancing. When Smith returned, he boasted to Powhatan that the English had defeated his Mannahoac enemies.

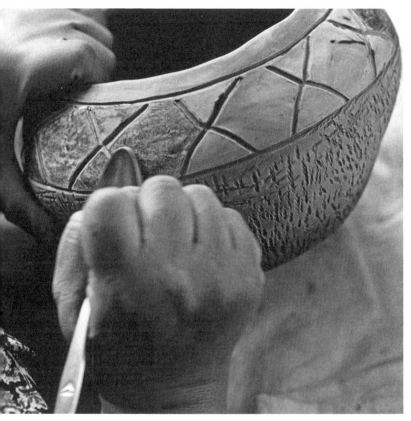

help at home or in the fields and could not finish even elementary school. Schools were operated for the tribes by the churches and were taught by white teachers. The Sappony Tribe received funding from North Carolina in 1911 for an Indian school; two years later, Sappony youth living on the Virginia side of the High Plains settlement were permitted to attend the school along with their fellow tribal members living on the North Carolina side.

High school education was not available to Indians in Virginia. Those who wished to attend were required to leave the state. A number of the Virginia Algonquian tribes sent their children to facilities such as the Bacone Indian School in Oklahoma, where they could complete high school and the equivalent of a community college degree. The trip to Bacone lasted 22 hours by train or bus, and children were rarely able to come home even for Christmas. Some of the graduates, such as Leonard and Marie Adkins, became teachers and leaders among their own people. About half of the Monacan families relocated during this time, many to Baltimore, Maryland. Meanwhile, students from tribes in faraway states such as North and South Dakota were being sent to Hampton Institute.

Public schooling was not made available to Virginia Indians until 1963, despite the decision of *Brown v. Board of Education* nine years earlier.

Beginning in the 1890s, many of the Virginia Algonquian tribes were visited by anthropologists James Mooney and later Frank Speck, who took photographs and compiled descriptions of their communities. With Speck's encouragement, the tribes attempted to revive the "Powhatan Confederacy" in the 1920s, and the first efforts toward organized political activism began. During the 1970s, various groups were organized, and tribes began working toward official state recognition. The Pamunkey Tribe successfully sued over a land claim involving reservation acreage they had lost during the Civil War. Eight tribes obtained official recognition from the Commonwealth in the 1980s, although the Pamunkey and Mattaponi had retained their reservations and had been observing their treaty relationship all along. The other state-recognized tribes are the Chickahominy, the Chickahominy Eastern Division, the Monacan, the Nansemond, the Rappahannock, and the Upper Mattaponi.

Among the Virginia Indian tribes, several traditional cultural forms are still practiced, and newer traditions have developed as well. Tribal artists work in beadwork, leather crafting, wood carving, pottery, and basket weaving. Tribal dancing continues, and Virginia Indians practice not only their own traditional dances, such as the Green Corn Dance and the Canoe Dance, but they also participate in intertribal powwow dancing as well. The Mattaponi and Pamunkey maintain fish hatcheries on their rivers to protect the population of American shad, and most tribes host an annual powwow as well as other public events.

Since the 1980s, the tribes have worked diligently to retain and reclaim our cultural traditions and improve economic conditions for our people. Chiefs are elected from among the tribal mem-

STATE RECOGNIZED TRIBES

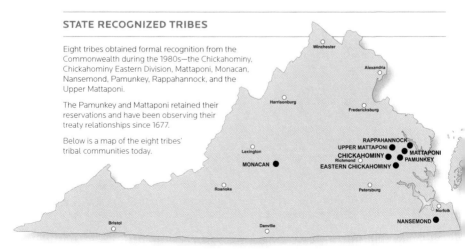

Eight tribes obtained formal recognition from the Commonwealth during the 1980s—the Chickahominy, Chickahominy Eastern Division, Mattaponi, Monacan, Nansemond, Pamunkey, Rappahannock, and the Upper Mattaponi.

The Pamunkey and Mattaponi retained their reservations and have been observing their treaty relationships since 1677.

Below is a map of the eight tribes' tribal communities today.

bers, and tribal councils meet regularly to address issues of concern and interest. Several tribes have established heritage classes for their young people and programs for elders. Almost all have purchased land in their homeland areas. Some are working on language reclamation. Six of the eight tribes have pursued federal acknowledgement through a bill introduced in Congress. Together the eight tribes worked to organize events for the Jamestown 2007 commemoration, and in 2006, fifty-five tribal delegates visited Kent County, England, where Pocahontas is buried. It was the first time a delegation of Virginia Indians had visited England in almost 400 years.

Virginia Indian people are justifiably proud of our history, our traditions, our survival, and our record of contributions to our state and country. We love our homelands, and we have fought to defend them over the centuries. We are made of this land, and we belong here. We come from this earth, this ground, and we will always be here.

THE LEGACY OF A COMPLEX ANNIVERSARY

by **DAVID BEARINGER**
Director of Grants and Public Programs
Virginia Foundation for the Humanities

We can assume that when the English came ashore in the place we now call Virginia in the spring of 1607, Chief Powhatan was not surprised. He would have known about earlier European attempts at settlement in the Mid-Atlantic; and the arrival of "a people from the East" had been foretold to him years before.

Powhatan was smart; he was prudent and a gifted military strategist. He was concerned about this invasion, probably from the first. The English were well armed, aggressive, and obviously in no rush to leave. It's easy to imagine his curiosity, mixed with heavy dollops of amusement and even disdain for these noisy, ill-prepared foreigners. But it's still a wonder that he spared the blustering John Smith—prophesy or no prophesy—and allowed the Jamestown colonists to live through their first winter in Virginia.

Clearly, this was his choice.

We can only guess the reasons why. But if Powhatan hadn't permitted it,

> The histories of Virginia's Indian communities are significant in their own right; they are also **essential, irreplaceable tributaries of the larger story of Virginia.**

Smith and his companions would almost surely never have emerged from the shadows of starvation and failure in the early years, or succeeded in establishing their fledgling colony, which to the Indians must have seemed as frail and tenuous as a hatchling sparrow.

The arguments are now persuasive that it was Powhatan's strength and imagination, even more than Smith's—the native people's forbearance even more than the settlers' tenacity and resourcefulness—that ultimately ensured Jamestown's survival. Should we honor Powhatan among the founders of Virginia?

The "New World" may have been new to the English. But it wasn't new

WHO WAS BEARSKIN?

In 1728, a Sappony Indian by the name of Bearskin accompanied the prominent colonist William Byrd, who was charged by the King of England to settle the border disputes between the colonies of North Carolina and Virginia. Byrd and about 30 woodsmen and traders ventured inland from the coastal plain through the swamps and dense woods. They soon realized the journey would be too long and difficult without the help of a guide to navigate and a skilled hunter to keep the large party fed.

Bearskin was chosen to accompany the surveying party because of his hunting acumen and knowledge of the Sappony territory. The boundary line that Bearskin helped to create runs through the Sappony Indian community, known today as the High Plains Indian Settlement. As a testament to Bearskin's skill and the many other proud Sappony people he met, William Byrd honored the Sappony by describing them as the bravest and most honest Indians he had ever known.

to Powhatan, or to the Mattaponi, the Pamunkey, the Nansemond, the Rappahannock, the Chickahominy, and the other tribes that comprised his paramount chiefdom and its allies. It wasn't new to the Monacan, the Saponi, the Meherrin, the Occaneechi, or the Patawomeke—to the 50,000 or more Native people living within the present-day boundaries of Virginia at the time the English arrived. And it wasn't new to millions of other Indians who by 1607 had formed complex, stable societies—keepers of faith, tradition, law, and vividly expressive cultures—from the Arctic Circle to Cape Horn.

Virginia's history is a complex web of stories, illustrious and painful. The Virginia Declaration of Rights was written here, but so were the infamous Racial Integrity laws that effectively denied to Indian people and to others in the state the right to claim their own identity.

The Bill of Rights, drafted by Virginians, has inspired people and nations throughout the world to assert the rights of individuals and place limits on the power of government. But for many decades, African Americans and Indians in the state were systematically denied their most basic rights and opportunities under Jim Crow segregation. Four of the first five U. S. presidents were from Virginia: all four were slave-owners. For more than two hundred years, the wealth and progress of Virginia were built in substantial part on slave labor. The colony and state of Virginia were established on Indian lands.

To the state's tremendous credit, the observance of Virginia's 400th anniversary in 2007 was more than simply a celebration. Indian people, along with many others, worked to make sure that this was so. One of the most important outcomes of 2007 was a sustained focus on the histories and cultures of Virginia Indians, and with it, a new level of recognition that Virginia Indians are not consigned to the distant past.

Equally important was the focus on Virginia's *complex* history; the recogni-

WHO WAS COCKACOESKE?

Cockacoeske was married to the Pamunkey chief Totopotomoy, who was killed in 1656 while fighting as an ally of the English at what became known as the Battle of Bloody Run. Following his death, she became the chief, or *weroansqua*, of the tribe. She was known to the English as the Queen of the Pamunkey. Despite their alliance with the English settlers, the Pamunkey were attacked by Nathaniel Bacon's forces during Bacon's Rebellion in 1676, and Cockacoeske was said to have barely escaped with her life.

Cockacoeske is best known for having signed the Articles of Peace, also called the Treaty of Middle Plantation in 1677—a treaty some historians believe she helped create, due to her ties with English officials governing the colony. This treaty placed her as leader over a number of Indian nations, including the Rappahannock and the Chickahominy, who had not previously been subject to the Powhatan paramount chiefdom. It also defined the Indian tribes as tributaries to the English and ushered in peaceful relations between the colonists and Indians of the Virginia coastal plain. Subsequent versions of the Articles of Peace were written over the next few years and signed by additional Indian nations.

Cockacoeske reigned until her death, about 1686, but her attempt to reestablish the paramount chiefdom failed, due to lack of cooperation among the tribes.

tion that within every chapter and page of this history, from the most inspiring to the most shameful, there are stories of survival, adaptation, persistence, creativity, and achievement that deserve to be told, and told again, in new ways.

Indian people in Virginia seized the opportunities of 2007 with enthusiasm and generosity. And as a result, non-Native Virginians and visitors to the state gained a much better understanding of Virginia Indian history and cultures in the present day, as well as of Indian perspectives on the shared history of the state.

The challenge for all of us, now that the moment of 2007 is past, is to continue deepening our common understanding of the "Virginia Experiment," of the forces Jamestown set in motion, of what Virginia has become and why; to celebrate what is good and worthy of celebration, and at the same time to acknowledge what's been lost, sacrificed, and forfeited, and by whom.

The histories of Virginia's Indian communities are significant in their own right; they are also essential, irreplaceable tributaries of the larger story of Virginia. This was true decades, even centuries before 2007, and it will remain true now that the observance of 2007 is past.

We are fortunate that portions of Virginia's Indian history and heritage are still accessible to all of us, through the resources that are included in this Heritage Trail guide. We are even more

fortunate that Virginia Indians are, in fact, still here, still able and willing to tell their own stories; that their cultures are living and changing, but still firmly intact, like trees with new foliage and thousand-year-old root systems.

All of us are richer because of this.

THE TRIBES OF VIRGINIA

During the 18th and 19th centuries, as English settlement encroached on the lands of Indian tribes in what came to be called Virginia, as disease and warfare took their toll on indigenous populations, and as repressive policies were instituted to regulate Indian ways of life, the tribes of Virginia were significantly reduced in number. Some indigenous groups left the area altogether, such as the Tutelo, who ended up in Canada, allied with their former enemies, the Haudenosaunee (Iroquois) confederacy. Other surviving groups banded together for protection against both the English and enemy tribes, and they remained in their homelands.

Today, eight tribes are officially recognized by the Commonwealth, but none is acknowledged by the federal government. How many groups exist in Virginia, such as the Patawomeke, without being formally acknowledged by the state? How many individuals trace their ancestry to Virginia Indian people of the past, without recognition, and how many people assert an Indian identity without validation from a tribal community? These are complicated questions.

In addition to the eight state-recognized tribes, other groups claiming Indian heritage make their homes in Virginia. A few tribes, such as the Meherrin, whose documented histories originate in Virginia, found themselves on the North Carolina side of the state line and are today recognized by the state of North Carolina. Three tribes of Saponi Indians—the Haliwa Saponi, the Sappony, and the Occaneechi Band of Saponi Indians[1]—are recognized by North Carolina, and their tribal headquarters are located not far from the Virginia state line. For indigenous peoples, boundary lines often exist arbitrarily and without reference to hundreds or thousands of years of Native history.

The Sappony, in particular, count 40 percent of their current population living in Virginia and 60 percent in North Carolina. Their territory at the time of English contact included much of the southern piedmont. Because the borderline runs through the heart of the Indian community, the tribe has continued its long-standing relationships with both governments in an effort to serve the Sappony Indian people who live on either side of the state line.

In 1607, the English documented thirty-two tribes belonging to Powhatan's paramount chiefdom. Today, only four of those tribes remain. Of the twenty-plus tribes belonging to the Siouan-speaking peoples of the piedmont and mountain regions, one remains in Virginia, two in North Carolina, and one on the state line between them. Nevertheless, our cultures are vibrant and thriving, testimony to the fortitude of our ancestors and our peoples' continuing determination to retain and reclaim our heritage.

[1] *This tribal name appears historically with various spellings, as do many others. Spellings used here reflect the choices of the three tribes, respectively.*

CHICKAHOMINY TRIBE

The Chickahominy Tribe is located in Charles City County, Virginia, midway between Richmond and Williamsburg, near where the tribe lived in 1600. When Jamestown was founded, the tribe lived in established villages along the Chickahominy River, from the mouth of the river near Jamestown to the middle of the current county of New Kent. Because of their proximity to Jamestown, the Chickahominy people had early contact with the English settlers, helping them to survive during their first few winters here by trading food for other items. Later, the tribal members helped teach the settlers how to grow and preserve their own food. Captain John Smith made several trade voyages up the Chickahominy River to the heart of the Chickahominy land.

8200 Lott Cary Road
Providence Forge, VA 23140
(804) 829-2027
www.chickahominyindiantribe.org

TRIBES

As the settlers began to prosper and expand their settlements, the Chickahominy were crowded out of their homeland. In the treaty of 1646, the tribe was granted reservation land in the Pamunkey Neck area of Virginia, near where the Mattaponi reservation now exists in King William County. Eventually, the tribe lost its reservation land, and the tribal families began a gradual migration to the area called the Chickahominy Ridge, where they now reside.

The families began to purchase land for their homes and established Samaria Baptist Church, which serves as an important focal point for the community. They also purchased land here for tribal use and eventually constructed a tribal center. Each year, the Fall Festival and Powwow is hosted by the tribe on its property near the tribal center, with people in attendance from all over the United States, particularly the East Coast.

At the time of the English colonists' arrival, the tribe was led by a council of elders and religious leaders called the *mungai* or "great men," rather than by a single person. Today, it is led by a tribal council consisting of twelve men and women, including a chief and two assistant chiefs, all elected by vote of the members of the tribe.

There are approximately 875 Chickahominy people living within a five-mile radius of the tribal center, with several hundred more living in other parts of the United States.

The Chickahominy Tribe was granted official recognition by the state of Virginia in 1983 and since 1996 has been working hard towards recognition by the federal government.

EASTERN CHICKAHOMINY TRIBE

The Chickahominy Tribe Eastern Division is located 25 miles east of Richmond in New Kent County, Virginia. European contact with the tribal ancestry of the modern-day Chickahominy Indians and the Chickahominy Indian Tribe Eastern Division is recorded as early as 1607. They shared a history until the early 1900s, when it was decided by the Eastern Chickahominy

3120 Mount Pleasant Road
Providence Forge, VA 23140
www.cied.org

to organize their own tribal government. This was done because of travel inconvenience to tribal meetings of the Chickahominy in Charles City County.

In 1910, a school was started in New Kent County for the Chickahominy Tribe Eastern Division. Grades 1 through 8 were taught in this one-room school. In 1920-21, the tribe was formally organized as a separate tribal government, with E.P. Bradby as the Chief. In September 1922 Tsena Commocko Indian Baptist Church was organized. Church services were held in the school building until a church could be built. In 1925, a certificate of incorporation was issued to the Chickahominy Tribe Eastern Division. The tribe presently has 132 members, with 67 members living in Virginia and the rest out of state.

The tribe is proud of its 26 veterans with service in the Armed Forces since World War I. Today the people of the tribe enjoy employment in the private sector, working in the areas of technology, nursing, business administration, and privately owned businesses.

The tribe purchased 41 acres of land in 2002, becoming one of the last of the eight state-recognized tribes in Virginia to own land. Tribal members plan to build a tribal center and museum, where functions can be held in an environment of fellowship and interaction with those who come from out of state. The hope to enrich and educate our people and the people of Virginia is a strong drive to move forward. The tribe currently holds meetings in the Tsena Commocko Baptist Church Fellowship Hall. The tribe was recognized by the

MATTAPONI INDIAN TRIBE

The members of this tribe live on a reservation that stretches along the borders of the Mattaponi River in King William County. The Mattaponi Indian Reservation dates back to 1658. In those early days, the people made their living completely from nature's resources. In 1646 the Mattaponi began paying tribute to an early Virginia governor. This practice continues to the present day, when on the fourth Wednesday of November the tribe presents game or fish to the governor of the Commonwealth of Virginia.

The Mattaponi Indian Reservation was created from land long held by the tribe by an act of the Virginia General Assembly in 1658. Being one of the oldest reservations in the country, the tribe traces its history back to the paramount chief Powhatan, father of Pocahontas, who ruled most of Tidewater Virginia when Europeans arrived in 1607. Since the Assembly's affirmation of the reservation in 1658, the Mattaponi Tribe has maintained its heritage and many of its customs despite strong pressures pushing toward assimilation with the mainstream culture.

Through the years, both the reservation's physical size and the number of tribal members have diminished. The reservation today encompasses approximately 150 acres, a portion of which is wetland. Although the Tribal Roll numbers 450 people, only 75 actually live on the reservation. The Mattaponi Indian Tribe is state recognized and continues to maintain its own sovereign government. The governing body today is made up of the chief, assistant chief, and seven councilmen. The mission of the Mattaponi people is to maintain a sustainable community on the Mattaponi River, a tributary of the Chesapeake Bay, that will extend the thousands of years of Mattaponi history

1467 Mattaponi Reservation Circle
West Point, VA 23181
www.baylink.org/mattaponi

and heritage and, in doing so, demonstrate to all people how they may live successful and rewarding lives in harmony with the earth. The reservation today sits on the banks of the Mattaponi River, one of the most pristine rivers in the Eastern United States. Facilities on the reservation include living quarters, a small church, a museum, the Fish Hatchery and Marine Science Facility, and a community tribal building that was formerly the reservation school.

Shad have always been a staple in the Mattaponi diet and at the center of the Mattaponi culture. The traditions continue as the Mattaponi people work in harmony with the land and the river. The Hatchery and Marine Science Facility were funded through grants from a number of foundations and organizations as well as from individual

contributions. The facility supports the tribe's traditional work with American shad and began several new programs that include fish tagging, water quality monitoring, and the development of educational materials for schools and communities about protecting water resources.

MONACAN INDIAN NATION

The Monacan Indian Nation is composed of about 1,600 tribal members, located in Amherst County and recognized as a tribe by the Commonwealth of Virginia on February 14, 1989. Native habitation in this region dates back more than 10,000 years, and the original territory of the tribe and its allies comprised more than half of the state of Virginia, including almost all of the Piedmont region and parts of the Blue Ridge Mountains. The Monacan Nation is one of the oldest groups of indigenous peoples still existing in their ancestral homeland, and the only group of Eastern Siouan people in the state.

Scientists believe that the Siouan-speaking people were unified at one time, thousands of years ago, in the Ohio River Valley, and that the tribes moved both east and west, separating into the Eastern and Western Siouan speakers. Monacan Indians spoke a language related to other Eastern Siouan tribes, such as the Tutelo. The Monacan are related to the Occaneechi and Saponi peoples now located in North Carolina, and they were affiliated with the Mannahoac, who occupied the northern Piedmont in Virginia.

Traditionally, Monacan people buried the remains of their dead in sacred earthen mounds constructed over time. Thirteen such mounds have been found throughout the Blue Ridge and Piedmont regions, similarly constructed, some more than a thousand years old. Thomas Jefferson observed several Indians visiting one of the mounds on his property in the 1700s. He later excavated the mound and became known as the father of American archaeology because he documented the findings.

P.O. Box 1136
Madison Heights, VA 24572
(434) 946-0389
www.monacannation.com

TRIBES

St. Paul's Episcopal Mission at Bear Mountain is the site of the tribe's ancestral museum and cultural center. The Episcopal Diocese returned the land on which the tribal center sits to the Monacan Nation in 1995, ending nearly a century of church control over this small tract held sacred by Monacan people. Since that time, the tribe has purchased more than 100 acres on Bear Mountain and has obtained two other parcels of land in the same area. Tribal members have begun a cultural education program, an elders' program, and a tribal scholarship fund. They have obtained numerous grants to fund their projects and have restored their log cabin schoolhouse, circa 1870, which is now a registered National Historic Landmark.

The tribe holds its Annual Powwow in May of each year and its Homecoming Festival on the first Saturday in October. Both events are open to the public.

NANSEMOND TRIBE

At the time of their first English contact in Virginia, the Nansemond Tribe lived in several villages along the Nansemond River centered near Chuckatuck, the current location of Suffolk. Their head chief lived near Dumpling Island, where the tribe's temples and sacred items were located. At that time, the tribe had a population of 1200 persons with 300 bowmen.

The arriving English raided the Nansemond town in 1608, burning their houses and destroying their canoes in order to force them to give up their corn, thus beginning the open hostilities between the two communities. As increasing numbers of Europeans poured into the Nansemond River area, the tribal members had to relocate their tribal lands and their reservation on several occasions, losing their last known reservation lands in 1792.

Currently most Nansemond tribal members still live in the Suffolk/Chesapeake area. The tribe holds its monthly meetings at the Indiana United Methodist Church, which was founded in 1850 as a mission for the Nansemond, and which is adjacent to the site of earlier tribal schools. The tribe was state recognized in 1985. The members have operated a tribal museum and gift shop in Chuckatuck, and they have current plans for a tribal center and museum and living history area on ancestral lands along the Nansemond River. They co-host a powwow each June with the city of Chesapeake, and they celebrate their tribal Annual Powwow each August.

P.O. Box 6558
Churchland Post Office
Portsmouth, VA 23703
www.nansemond.org

TRIBES

PAMUNKEY TRIBE

The Pamunkey Indian Reservation, on the Pamunkey River and adjacent to King William County, contains approximately 1,200 acres, 500 acres of which is wetlands with many creeks. Thirty-one families reside on the reservation, and many tribal members live in nearby Richmond and Newport News, as well as throughout Virginia and the U.S.

The history of the Pamunkey Tribe has been recorded by archaeologists, anthropologists, and historians, and Native occupation of their tribal area dates back ten to twelve thousand years. Opechancanough was the chief of the Pamunkey, and he succeeded Powhatan as paramount chief shortly after Powhatan's death. Modern-day Pamunkey Indians are descendants of Opechancanough's and Powhatan's people. Legal acknowledgment came with the 1646 and 1677 treaties with the King of England. The Articles of Peace between Lord Charles II and several Virginia Indian tribes were signed on behalf of the tribes by the head woman of the Pamunkey, Cockacoeske, at the camp at Middle Plantation on May 20, 1677. The two major treaties with the Pamunkey established Articles of Peace and a land base as early as 1658.

Pamunkey Tribal Government
175 Lay Landing Road
King William, VA 23086
(804) 512-3363
www.baylink.org/pamunkey

TRIBES

This is the reservation that exists today.

The tribe has maintained its own governing body, which consists of a chief and seven council members elected every four years. The chief and council perform all tribal governmental functions as set forth by their laws. All of these laws are administered by the tribe itself.

Elections are held every four years, in the traditional manner of using a pea and a corn. A basket is passed around on election night with the same number of peas and corn kernels as voters. The chief is the first to be voted on, and then the seven councilmen. Each person is given a pea and a corn to vote when the basket is passed for a candidate. A corn is for a "yes" vote for the candidate, and a pea is for a "no" vote. The peas and corn are counted for each person. Finally, when the basket has been passed for each candidate for the position, the person with the most corn is elected.

The Pamunkey have some unique dealings with the state and federal governments. Public Law 96-484 acknowledges the Pamunkey as a tribe covered by the Non-Intercourse Act. House Report No. 96-1144, PW, states that "both Federal and State prohibit the acquisition of Pamunkey tribal lands without the consent of the Federal and State governments." The "Indian Tribal Government Tax Status Act," 26 U.S.C. §7871, which extends to tribal governments numerous tax advantages that have been enjoyed by states and their subdivisions, applies to the Pamunkey Tribe. Pamunkey people have served in the U.S. Armed Services during every war and major conflict, beginning with the Revolutionary War.

RAPPAHANNOCK TRIBE

The Rappahannock probably first encountered the English in 1603. It was likely Captain Samuel Mace who sailed up the Rappahannock River and was befriended by the Rappahannock chief. The record tells us that the ship's captain killed the chief and took a group of Rappahannock men back to England. In December 1603, those men were documented giving dugout demonstrations on the Thames River. In December 1607, the Rappahannock people first met Captain John Smith at their capital town "Topahanocke," on the banks of the river bearing their name. At the time, Smith was a prisoner of Powhatan's war chief, Opechancanough. He took Smith to the Rappahannock town for the people to determine whether Smith was the Englishman who, four years earlier, had murdered their chief and kidnapped some of their people. Smith was found innocent of these crimes, at least, and he returned to the Rappahannock homeland in the summer of 1608, when he mapped 14 Rappahannock towns on the north side of the river. The territory on the south side of the river was the primary Rappahannock hunting ground.

English settlement in the Rappahannock River valley began illegally in the 1640s. After Bacon's Rebellion, the Rappahannock consolidated into one village, and in November 1682 the Virginia Council laid out 3,474 acres for the Rappahannock in Indian Neck, where their descendants live today. One year later, the Virginia colony forcibly removed the tribal members from their homes and relocated them, to be used as a human shield to protect white Virginians from the Iroquois of New York, who continued to attack the Virginia frontier and to threaten the expansion of English settlement.

Rappahannock Cultural Center
5036 Indian Neck Rd.
Indian Neck, VA 23148
(804) 769-0260
e-mail · www.rappahannocktribe@aol.com
web · www.rappahannocktribe.org

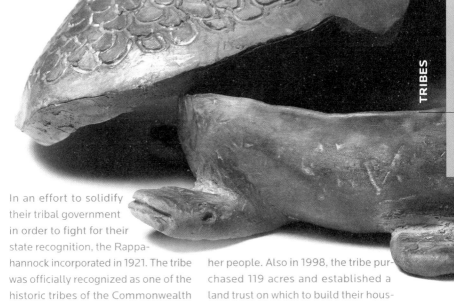

TRIBES

In an effort to solidify their tribal government in order to fight for their state recognition, the Rappahannock incorporated in 1921. The tribe was officially recognized as one of the historic tribes of the Commonwealth of Virginia by an act of the General Assembly on March 25, 1983. In 1996 the Rappahannock reactivated work on federal acknowledgment, which had begun in 1921, when Chief George Nelson petitioned the U.S. Congress to recognize Rappahannock civil and sovereign rights. In 1995 they began construction of their cultural center project and completed two phases by 1997. In 1998 the Rappahannock tribe elected the first woman chief, G. Anne Richardson, to lead a tribe in Virginia since the 1700s. As a fourth-generation chief in her family, she brings to the position a long legacy of traditional leadership and service among

her people. Also in 1998, the tribe purchased 119 acres and established a land trust on which to build their housing development. They built their first home and sold it in 2001.

The Rappahannock Tribe hosts their traditional Harvest Festival and Pow-wow annually on the second Saturday in October at their Cultural Center in Indian Neck. They have a traditional dance group called the Rappahannock Native American Dancers and a drum group called the Maskapow Drum Group, which means "Little Beaver" in the Powhatan language. Both of these groups perform locally and abroad in their efforts to educate the public about Rappahannock history and tradition.

UPPER MATTAPONI TRIBE

For centuries the ancestors of the Upper Mattaponi people lived in villages along the waterways of Virginia. They harvested corn, beans, and squash and hunted deer. They spoke an Algonquian language, and when the British came in 1607 they were prosperous members of the Powhatan paramount chiefdom. Captain John Smith's map of 1612 indicates that the tribe's present location corresponds with a village called Passaunkack.

In the mid-1600s, the upper reaches of the Mattaponi River were still frontier, and other tribes had been forced into the area by the expansion of the British. A 1673 map drawn by August Hermann notes the largest concentration of Indians near Passaunkack, home of the Upper Mattaponi. The Peace Treaty of 1677 was signed on behalf of the Mattaponi by Werowansqua Cockacoeske, and a reservation of Chickahominy and Mattaponi was established near Passaunkack. During the 1700s, the Chickahominy moved back to their homeland. Those people who remained were the ancestors of today's Upper Mattaponi Tribe.

13383 King William Road
King William, VA 23086
www.uppermattaponi.org

Through the 18th and 19th centuries, the Upper Mattaponi were known as the Adamstown Band, because so many of the tribal citizens had the last name Adams. By 1850 a nucleus of at least 10 Adamstown families were documented in the area, farming and hunting. A Civil War map of 1863 designated the area as Indian Land, and by the 1880s the Adamstown Band had built its own school. Because of the racial climate, Indian people had few rights and found it difficult to prosper. Even so, they valued an education, and the first federal funds were requested in 1892 for education of the Adamstown Indians. In the early 20th century, a cultural revival spread throughout the tribes of the region, and the band changed its name to the Upper Mattaponi Indian Tribe.

In 1919 the tribe built a small one-room schoolhouse, Sharon Indian School. This building served them until 1952, when a brick structure was erected adjacent to the original building. The new school was closed in 1965 with the policy of desegregation, and it is now on the Virginia Landmarks Register and the National Register of Historic Buildings. It is the only public Indian school building still existing in Virginia. Today Sharon Indian School is used for events such as tribal meetings and cultural gatherings.

By the 1800s, most Upper Mattaponi people had converted to Christianity and worshipped in their homes or in other Indian churches, in particular the Pamunkey and Mattaponi reservation churches. In the early 20th century, church services were held in the one-room school building, but in 1942 the tribe built a new church, Indian View Baptist. Every summer, homecoming is held on the grounds, and hundreds of Upper Mattaponi and dozens of Indians from other Virginia tribes join together there.

During the last half of the 20th century, even as the Upper Mattaponi people maintained their tribal identity, they became part of the fabric of mainstream America as physicians, pharmacists, accountants and business owners. The tribe has purchased land, where many cultural events are held, and they have plans to develop a new tribal center.

GUIDE TO THE SITES

From 2005 through early 2007, Virginia Indian Heritage Trail researchers visited more than 100 sites throughout Virginia that offer interpretive exhibits and programs about Virginia Indians. These were sites that responded to the "Time Travelers (Before 1607)" program of the Virginia Association for Museums and selected others. Each site was analyzed for historical accuracy, cultural sensitivity, and completeness of presentation. Our researchers then made recommendations as to whether each site should be included in this guide and why. The recom-

mendations were shared with the chiefs and assistant chiefs of the eight state-recognized tribes and with the Virginia Council on Indians, an advisory Council to the Governor and state legislature, whose members represent the state tribes and the at-large Indian population. The sites included here result from that selection process.

We found that site presentations are generally more accurate than we might have expected, and attempts are being made to update facilities and exhibits through-

Information listed in this guide is current as of publication, but we suggest contacting sites before visiting.

out the Commonwealth. Unfortunately, we also found that many presentations focus heavily on archaeological discoveries, with arrowheads and potsherds being relatively common and interpretative material focusing only on "prehistoric" periods. Virginia Indian history seems to end around 1700, according to some presentations, and in a number of exhibits there is no connection between Indian peoples of the past and present.

At the same time, there appears to be a renaissance within some Virginia museums and other sites, with an expanded interpretation emphasizing the continuing history and contributions of Virginia Indians into the present day. We are beginning to tell a more complete story, a more interesting story. In this way, we can all learn more about who we are.

KEY TO **HISTORICAL ERAS**

A **Pre-Contact**
10,000 BCE-1607

B **Early Contact and Settlement**
1607-1622

C **Conflict, Reservations, and Treaties**
1622-1699

D **Pre-Revolution**
1700-1776

E **Revolution**
1776-1785

F **Indians and the Creation of the U.S.**
1785-1820s

G **Jackson and Removal**
1820-1840s

H **Civil War and After**
1860-1880

I **Darwin, Plecker and Eugenics**
1880-1970s

J **Fight for Recognition**
1980-present

TRIBAL
SITES

Mattaponi Indian Reservation

Museum, Shad Fish Hatchery,
Pottery Shop, and Trading Post
Mattaponi Tribal Government
Rt. 2, Box 255
West Point, VA 23181

COUNTY   King William
EMAIL   *leagle@inna.net*
WEBSITE *www.baylink.org/Mattaponi*
CONTACT Gertrude Custalow, Director

TYPE OF HERITAGE SITE
Reservation, Museum /Cultural Center

HISTORICAL ERAS

A	**Pre-Contact**	10,000 BCE-1607
B	**Early Contact and Settlement**	1607-1622
C	**Conflict, Reservations, and Treaties**	1622-1699
D	**Pre-Revolution**	1700-1776
E	Revolution	1776-1781
F	Indians and the Creation of the U.S.	1781-1820
G	Jackson and Removal	1820-1860
H	Civil War and After	1860-1880
I	Darwin, Plecker and Eugenics	1880-1930
J	Fight for Recognition	1930-present

TRIBAL SITES

HISTORICAL SIGNIFICANCE

The Museum contains exhibits covering the Ice Age, Paleolithic, Archaic, and Woodland time periods. Tribal history, stone tools, bowls, and newspaper clippings are some of the items available at the Museum. Additionally, the history of the Annual Tax Tribute, presented by the Mattaponi and Pamunkey Tribes to the Virginia Governor in honor of the 1646 Treaty, is available covering the period from the late 1800s to the present. The shad hatchery presents information on river ecology and recovery efforts, which include the hatching and releasing of fingerling shad into the Mattaponi River. The Pottery Shop offers visitors a glimpse of the continuing Mattaponi pottery tradition, and the Trading Post offers items for sale.

PHYSICAL DESCRIPTION

Located in the north central area of the Middle Peninsula, on the Mattaponi River, this is one of two Indian reservations in Virginia.

DIRECTIONS From Richmond, Rt. 360 East. Turn right on Rt. 30. Turn onto State Rt. 626 and turn left. Follow signs onto the Reservation.

HOURS   Saturday and Sunday 10–4. Available by appointment other days.
ADMISSION $2.50 per person

Handicapped accessible, restrooms, brochures

Pamunkey Reservation

Pamunkey Tribal Government
175 Lay Landing Road
King William, VA 23086

COUNTY   King William
WEBSITE   *www.baylink.org/Pamunkey*
CONTACT   Chief Kevin Brown, (804) 512-3363

TYPE OF HERITAGE SITE
Reservation, Museum /Cultural Center

HISTORICAL ERAS

A	Pre-Contact 10,000 BCE-1607
B	Early Contact and Settlement 1607-1622
C	Conflict, Reservations, and Treaties 1622-1699
D	Pre-Revolution 1700-1776
E	Revolution 1776-1785
F	Indians and the Creation of the U.S. 1785-1820s
G	Jackson and Removal 1820-1840s
H	Civil War and After 1860-1880
I	Darwin, Plecker and Eugenics 1880-1920s
J	Fight for Recognition 1980-present

HISTORICAL SIGNIFICANCE

This museum has one of the finest collections of replicated artifacts in the U.S. Many of the pieces were made by some of the best flint-knappers in the world. The museum was created in consultation with Dr. Errett Callahan, who conducted research with the Pamunkey in the 1970s and 1980s. Exhibits cover the Ice Age, Paleolithic, Archaic, and Woodland time periods. Additional topics covered include pottery making, a continuous tradition since pre-contact times (though styles have reflected more modern techniques over the past 100 years). Other exhibits discuss more recent events and past chiefs during the last 100 years.

PHYSICAL DESCRIPTION

The Reservation is located adjacent to the Pamunkey River in the central Middle Peninsula. It is one of two Indian reservations in the state.

DIRECTIONS   From Richmond, Rt. 360 East. Turn right onto Rt. 30. Turn right on Rt. 633 (Powhatan Trail). Turn right on Rt. 673. Once on the Reservation, follow signs to museum.

HOURS   Tuesday–Saturday 10–4; Sunday 1–4.
ADMISSION $2.50 per person, $1.50 for seniors

Handicapped accessible, restrooms, brochures

Pamunkey Indian Museum and Historical Sites

To walk through the museum is to walk through time. Beginning with the Ice Age, you are made familiar with "The People" (what they looked like, their ornaments, and their existence); "Their Natural Environment" (the land they inhabited, and how it looked); "Their Settlement" (the dwelling places of the people); and "Their Subsistence" (the tools they used and how they survived). These four themes reappear in each archaeological time frame shown. Also, there are three documentary films about reservation life.

One of the most important buildings on the reservation is the Tribal Council complex, and the least conspicuous is the Pottery School. Set off by itself at the edge of the woods, it has been the home of the Pamunkey Indian Potters' Guild since the early 1930s. Clay has been dug from the shores of the Pamunkey River on the reservation for hundreds of years. The clay is used today by the current potters, who still use the ancient method of coiling to make their pottery. In addition, pit firing is still practiced by contemporary Pamunkey potters using wood and bark to fire the pottery and other items. The Museum shop glitters with the crafts that attest to the industry of the cooperative's members. All people are welcome to visit the museum and the Pamunkey Reservation.

The Pamunkey Baptist Church is the oldest Indian church in the state. It was built by tribal members in 1865 and still has Sunday school and morning services every Sunday.

After many years of Pamunkey Chiefs petitioning the Governor's office to provide a school for the children of the reservation, a one-room schoolhouse was built by members of the tribe with help from the Commonwealth of Virginia. Grades 1 through 7 were offered at the school, which was attended by both Pamunkey and Mattaponi children. For years, the Pamunkey children could only go as high as the 7th grade in the reservation school. In later years, they had to travel hundreds of miles to attend one of the BIA boarding schools in order to obtain a high school education.

A visit to the Pamunkey Shadfish Hatchery allows one to see the embodiment of a sustained effort to preserve and restore the American Shad, one of the Chesapeake Bay's indigenous species, which travel the Pamunkey River each spring to spawn. Since 1918, the Hatchery has been hatching and releasing fingerling shad into the river during the spawning season. The Pamunkey have maintained a philosophy that if you took fish from the water, you should put some back. In this way we honor the traditions of our ancestors.

TRIBAL SITES

Rappahannock Tribal Center

Rappahannock Tribal Center
5036 Indian Neck Road
Indian Neck, VA 23148

COUNTY   King & Queen
PHONE   (804) 769-0260
EMAIL   *info@rappahannocktribe.org*
WEBSITE   *www.rappahannocktribe.org*

TYPE OF HERITAGE SITE
Museum /Cultural Center

HISTORICAL ERAS

A	**Pre-Contact**	*10,000 BCE-1607*
B	**Early Contact and Settlement**	*1607-1622*
C	**Conflict, Reservations, and Treaties**	*1622-1699*
D	**Pre-Revolution**	*1700-1776*
E	Revolution	*1776-1785*
F	Indians and the Creation of the U.S.	*1785-1820*
G	Jackson and Removal	*1820-1840s*
H	Civil War and After	*1860-1880*
I	**Darwin, Plecker and Eugenics**	*1880-1970s*
J	Fight for Recognition	*1990-present*

HISTORICAL SIGNIFICANCE

The tribal museum contains both modern and prehistoric items (points, pottery, etc.), including items from past archaeological digs. A set of beads from early contact are on site and are a significant find. These trade beads would have been introduced in the early 1600s. Historical photographs of tribal members are present. One in particular shows a rabbit hunt and the use of "rabbit sticks" from the 1930s or 1940s. Tribal members are available to provide historical information. A facial reconstruction of an early Rappahannock man has recently been added to the displays, along with educational materials.

PHYSICAL DESCRIPTION

The Tribal Center is adjacent to the grounds where an annual one-day powwow is held.

DIRECTIONS From Richmond, Rt. 360 East. In King & Queen County, turn left on Newton Rd. After 3 miles, turn right at Owens Mill Rd. Turn right onto Indian Neck Rd. Tribal center is on left.

HOURS   By appointment
ADMISSION None

Handicapped accessible, restrooms, brochures

Monacan Ancestral Museum

Monacan Indian Nation
2009 Kenmore Road
Amherst, VA 24521

COUNTY Amherst
PHONE (434) 946-5391; (434) 946-0389
EMAIL *MNation538@aol.com*
WEBSITE *www.monacannation.com/museum.shtml*
CONTACT Sue Elliot, Director

TYPE OF HERITAGE SITE
Church; Educational Site, Museum /Cultural Center

HISTORICAL ERAS

A Pre-Contact
10,000 BCE-1607

Early Contact and Settlement
1607-1622

Conflict, Reservations, and Treaties
1622-1699

Pre-Revolution
1699-1776

Revolution
1776-1785

F Indians and the Creation of the U.S.
1785-1820s

G Jackson and Removal
1820-1840s

H Civil War and After
1860-1880

I Darwin, Plecker and Eugenics
1880-1970s

J Fight for Recognition
1980-present

TRIBAL SITES

HISTORICAL SIGNIFICANCE

The Museum houses hundreds of artifacts, including archaic projectile points, pottery, 18th- and 19th-century household items, and contemporary basketry and crafts. Visitors can watch a 20-minute video produced by a tribal member about Monacan history. Along with hundreds of photographs of tribal members over the past two centuries, the Museum also showcases two facial reproductions of ancestral Monacan Indians, created using forensic techniques. It offers T-shirts, books, and other items for sale.

Adjacent to the Museum is the restored log cabin mission schoolhouse, circa 1870, which is now a National Historic Landmark. This one-room schoolhouse served as the only source of education for Monacan people until 1964. It is open to the public and contains items from the past century. St. Paul's Episcopal Church, est. 1907, is still in use.

PHYSICAL DESCRIPTION
The Monacan Ancestral Museum is at the foot of Bear Mountain, the traditional center of the Monacan Tribe.

DIRECTIONS From Charlottesville, Rt. 29 South to third Amherst exit (Rt. 29 Business North). Left on Kenmore Rd. The museum is about 6 winding miles on the left.

HOURS Tuesday–Saturday 9–3 or by appointment.
Please call ahead to verify that staff is available.

ADMISSION $3 per person

Handicapped accessible, restrooms, brochures

INTERPRETIVE
SITES

Gulf Branch Nature Center

3608 N. Military Rd.
Arlington, VA 22207

COUNTY	Arlington
PHONE	(703) 228-3403
WEBSITE	*www.arlingtonva.us/Departments/ ParksRecreation/scripts/nature/ ParksRecreationScriptsNatureGulfbranch.aspx*

TYPE OF HERITAGE SITE
County Park

HISTORICAL ERAS

 Pre-Contact
10,000 BCE-1607

Early Contact and Settlement
1607-1622

Conflict, Reservations, and Treaties
1622-1699

Pre-Revolution
1700-1775

Revolution
1775-1795

Indians and the Creation of the U.S.
1795-1820

Jackson and Removal
1820-1840

Civil War and After
1840-1880

Darwin, Plecker and Eugenics
1880-1920

Fight for Recognition
1920-present

HISTORICAL SIGNIFICANCE

This park offers various exhibits, including a small collection of Woodland arti-facts and descriptive interpretation focused on pre-contact Native life in the area: foods, tools, pottery, and natural environment.

PHYSICAL DESCRIPTION

Located on 38 acres at the site of Gulf Branch stream, with pond, wooded trails and access to the Potomac River. The park, primarily wooded, is a good place to study native woodland plant communities. The center has an interpretive nature center, a recon-structed log house, a blacksmith's shop, animal displays, and educational programs offered year round.

DIRECTIONS The Nature Center is located in North Arlington. From Lee Highway, turn North onto Military Rd. Pass through two lights. After the second light, the driveway for the nature center is at the bottom of the second hill. Look for the brown signs.

Public Transportation: Orange metro line to Ballston or to East Falls Church. Then take ART 53—it stops in front of park driveway, between 36th and 37th Rd.

HOURS Tuesday–Saturday 10–5; Sunday 1–5; closed Mondays

ADMISSION Free

Not handicapped accessible; restrooms, brochures

INTERPRETIVE SITES

Leesylvania State Park

2001 Daniel K. Ludwig Drive
Woodbridge, VA 22191

COUNTY — Prince William County
PHONE — (703) 730-8205
EMAIL — *leesylvania@dcr.virginia.gov*
WEBSITE — *www.dcr.virginia.gov/state_parks/lee.shtml*

TYPE OF HERITAGE SITE
Historic Park/Natural Area

HISTORICAL ERAS

A — **Pre-Contact** *10,000 BCE-1607*
B — **Early Contact and Settlement** *1607-1622*
C — **Conflict, Reservations, and Treaties** *1622-1699*
Pre-Revolution *1700-1775*
Revolution *1775-1785*
Indians and the Creation of the U.S. *1785-1820s*
Jackson and Removal *1820-1840s*
Civil War and After *1850-1880*
Darwin, Plecker and Eugenics *1880-1970s*
Fight for Recognition *1980-present*

HISTORICAL SIGNIFICANCE

The display at Leesylvania is small but has a great deal of information. It is composed of a small number of artifacts and several reproductions by Daniel Abbott and Kelly Viars. The display contains pictures including the John Smith map of 1612 and John White drawings with descriptions. Periods covered are Paleo, Archaic, and Woodland. Several small informative displays describe the Powhatan paramount chiefdom and the Dogue Indians.

PHYSICAL DESCRIPTION

A 500-acre park on a peninsula bordered by the Potomac River, Neabsco Creek and Powells Creek, with hiking trails, a public beach and boat ramp.

DIRECTIONS — From Fredericksburg, take I-95 South to Rippon Landing exit 156. Head east on Rt. 784 to U.S. Rt. 1, then head east on Rt. 610 (Neabsco Rd.) 2 miles to park entrance.

HOURS — Dawn till dusk
ADMISSION — $4 parking fee weekdays, $5 on weekends & holidays

Handicapped accessible, restrooms, brochures

King William Historical Museum

227 Horse Landing Road
P.O. Box 233
King William, VA 23086

COUNTY   King William
PHONE   (804) 769-9619
WEBSITE   *www.kingwilliamcounty.us/museum.htm*

TYPE OF HERITAGE SITE
Museum/Cultural Center

HISTORICAL ERAS

A	**Pre-Contact** 10,000 BCE-1607
B	**Early Contact and Settlement** 1607-1622
C	Conflict, Reservations, and Treaties 1622-1705
D	Pre-Revolution 1700-1775
E	Revolution 1775-1783
F	Indians and the Creation of the U.S 1783-1830s
G	Jackson and Removal 1810s-1840s
H	Civil War and After 1860-1900
I	Darwin, Plecker and Eugenics 1900-1950s
J	Fight for Recognition 1950s-2000s

INTERPRETIVE SITES

HISTORICAL SIGNIFICANCE

The museum features displays including Virginia Indian, African American, and colonial artifacts; a timeline that spans 1607 to present; an Aylett port scene, and a King William mural. Virginia Indian exhibits were developed in consultation with tribal leaders, who served on the advisory board.

PHYSICAL DESCRIPTION

Located in the old Circuit Court Clerk's office on the Courthouse Green.

DIRECTIONS   From Richmond, Rt. 360 east to Rt. 30 east. Follow Rt. 30 into King William. Courthouse Green is on the left.

HOURS   Saturday 10–5, Sunday 1–5 or by appointment.
ADMISSION   Free, donations accepted.

Restrooms. Tours of the original Courthouse are also available.

Richmond County Museum

5874 Richmond Road
Warsaw, VA 22572

COUNTY   Richmond
PHONE   (804) 333-3607
EMAIL   *museum@co.richmond.va.us*
WEBSITE   *www.co.richmond.va.us/museum.htm*
CONTACT   Francine Barber, David Jett

TYPE OF HERITAGE SITE
Museum/Cultural Center

HISTORICAL ERAS

A	**Pre-Contact**	*10,000 BCE-1607*
B	**Early Contact and Settlement**	*1607-1622*
C	**Conflict, Reservations, and Treaties**	*1622-1699*
D	Pre-Revolution	*1700-1776*
E	Revolution	*1776-1785*
F	Indians and the Creation of the U.S.	*1785-1820s*
G	Jackson and Removal	*1820-1940s*
H	Civil War and After	*1860-1880*
I	**Darwin, Plecker and Eugenics**	*1880-1970s*
J	**Fight for Recognition**	*1980-present*

HISTORICAL SIGNIFICANCE

Exhibits developed in consultation with the Rappahannock Tribe tell the story of the tribe from pre-colonial times through display panels and an interaction time-line. Lithic objects are featured, as well as more recent items, such as oak splint baskets and a bread tray. A photo exhibit details the involvement of anthropologist Frank Speck with the tribe, circa 1920. Contemporary Rappahannock activities are also discussed. An excellent exhibit on the pottery of Mattaponi tribal members June and Ernest Langston is unique.

PHYSICAL DESCRIPTION

Located in the historic jail house, circa 1872, on the Courthouse Green.

DIRECTIONS   From Richmond, Rt. 360 east through Tappahannock and across Rappahannock River to town of Warsaw. The museum is on the right.
From Fredericksburg, Rt. 3 east to intersection of Rt. 360, turn right on 360, and museum is on left.

HOURS   Open Wednesday–Saturday 11–3 and by appointment.
Closed December–February.
ADMISSION   Free, donations accepted.

Not handicapped accessible, but 1st floor has wheelchair access.
Restrooms, brochures. Guided tours available.

Barrier Islands Center

The Eastern Shore of Virginia Barrier Islands Center
P.O. Box 206
Machipongo, VA 23405

COUNTY	Accomac
PHONE	(757) 678-5550; Toll free: (888) 678-5572
EMAIL	*bic@esva.net*
WEBSITE	*www.barrierislandscenter.com*
CONTACT	Dr. Harry Holcomb, Curator

TYPE OF HERITAGE SITE
Museum /Cultural Center

HISTORICAL ERAS

A   **Pre-Contact**
10,000 BCE-1607

B   **Early Contact and Settlement**
1607-1622

Conflict, Reservations, and Treaties
1622-1699

Pre-Revolution
1700-1776

Revolution
1776-1785

Indians and the Creation of the U.S.
1785-1820s

Jackson and Removal
1820-1840s

Civil War and After
1860-1880

Darwin, Plecker and Eugenics
1880-1970s

Fight for Recognition
1980-present

INTERPRETIVE SITES

HISTORICAL SIGNIFICANCE

The Center has a small exhibit of artifacts showcasing the indigenous inhabitants of the Eastern Shore before contact. There are about 30 pieces in this lithic collection, mainly projectile points and bifaces. There is also an exhibit about John Smith's winter stay on the shore in 1608, which briefly discusses the Native people he encountered. Exhibits are well lit, well crafted, and neatly arranged. Throughout the year, there are activities and lectures; topics have included Eastern Shore ecology and Native inhabitants.

PHYSICAL DESCRIPTION
Housed in a turn-of-the-century building with bookstore and gift shop.

DIRECTIONS   From the south, the site is 20 minutes north of the toll booth on the Chesapeake Bay Bridge Tunnel. Turn left onto Young St. and into the driveway. Located between mile markers 90 and 91 on Rt. 13.

HOURS   Tuesday–Saturday 10–4; Sunday 1–5
ADMISSION   None

Handicapped accessible, restrooms, brochures

Brafferton Indian School

College of William and Mary
Wren Building Offices
Williamsburg, VA 23187

COUNTY	City of Williamsburg
PHONE	(757) 221-1540
WEBSITE	*www.wm.edu*
CONTACT	Louis Kale, Director of Programs

HISTORICAL ERAS

A	Pre-Contact 10,000 BCE-1607
B	Early Contact and Settlement 1607-1622
C	**Conflict, Reservations, and Treaties** **1622-1699**
D	**Pre-Revolution** **1700-1776**
E	**Revolution** **1776-1785**
F	Indians and the Creation of the U.S. 1785-1820s
G	Jackson and Removal 1820-1840s
H	Civil War and After 1860-1880
I	Darwin, Plecker and Eugenics 1880-1970s
J	Fight for Recognition 1980-present

TYPE OF HERITAGE SITE

Educational Site (*NOTE: The Brafferton and the President's house are not open to the public. The Wren Building offers interpretive panels and historical overviews of the campus.*)

HISTORICAL SIGNIFICANCE

The Brafferton building, located on the south side of the Wren yard, was constructed in 1723 to house the College's Indian school, which was endowed by funds from the estate of Robert Boyle, the noted English scientist. Income from Brafferton Manor in Yorkshire, England, designated for charitable and pious purposes, was used to educate and prepare American Indian boys for Anglican priesthood. Local interest maintained the school for political purposes as well, creating cultural liaisons and interpreters for the British Empire, expanding its colonial borders. Members of the Pamunkey, Nansemond, Nottoway, Meherrin, Catawba, Cherokee, Chickahominy, Sappony/Occaneechee, Wyandot, and Delaware were included at various times on the school's rolls. This undertaking met with varying degrees of success. At the time of the Revolution, income from the Boyle estate was discontinued, and the Indian school was abandoned.

PHYSICAL DESCRIPTION

Inside the Wren building is a Brafferton panel, across from the chapel. There are also main panels of historical information in the foyer. Exterior panels highlight the mission of the school and its dedication to the Native people.

DIRECTIONS	From I-64, exit at Colonial Williamsburg exit and turn right on Rt. 132. Cross Rt. 60. Follow signs to downtown Williamsburg. The College's entrance is across from Merchant Square. The Wren is the main building, flanked on the left by the Brafferton (between Jamestown and Richmond Roads).
HOURS	Wren Building, Weekdays 10–5; Saturdays 9–5; Sundays 12–5
ADMISSION	Free. For free guided tours of the Wren building, call (757) 221-1540.

Handicapped accessible, restrooms, brochures, guided tours

First Landing State Park

2500 Shore Drive
Virginia Beach, VA 23451

COUNTY	City of Virginia Beach
PHONE	(757) 412-2300
EMAIL	*firstlanding@dcr.virginia.gov*
WEBSITE	*www.dcr.virginia.gov/state_parks/fir.shtml*
CONTACT	Staci Martin

TYPE OF HERITAGE SITE
Historic Park/Natural Area

HISTORICAL ERAS

A	**Pre-Contact** 10,000 BCE–1607
B	**Early Contact and Settlement** 1607–1622
C	**Conflict, Reservations, and Treaties** 1622–1699
D	Pre-Revolution 1700–1776
E	Revolution 1776–1788
F	Indians and the Creation of the U.S. 1765–1820s
G	Jackson and Removal 1820–1840s
H	Civil War and After 1860–1880
I	Darwin, Plecker and Eugenics 1880–1970s
J	Fight for Recognition 1880–present

HISTORICAL SIGNIFICANCE

This is the site of the first landing of the English colonists in 1607, who went on upriver to found Jamestown. Interpretive panels in the Chesapeake Bay Center address interaction between Powhatan Indians and English, as well as Powhatan lifestyles at contact, and they encourage visitors to ask questions; they also compare English and Powhatan cultures in ways that are favorable to both. Additional panels describe wildlife and the environment and how they have changed. Across the road, pre-colonial Powhatan-style structures have been newly created with assistance from Nansemond tribal members and academic experts, featuring a Powhatan home, a sweat lodge and a temple. There is also an Indian fishing and hunting camp. The site is part of a half-mile paved walking and bike trail incorporated into the 6-mile Cape Henry Trail.

PHYSICAL DESCRIPTION

Beautiful location at the confluence of the Chesapeake Bay and Atlantic Ocean, north of the Virginia Beach oceanfront and tourist area.

DIRECTIONS	From I-64, take Northampton Blvd./U.S. 13 North (Exit 282). Go through eight lights, then turn right at the Shore Drive/U.S. 60 exit (last exit before the Chesapeake Bay Bridge Tunnel). Take a right on Shore Drive and go four and a half miles to the park entrance. To reach the Chesapeake Bay Center, park office, camping or cabins, turn left off U.S. Rt. 60 at the stoplight and check in at the contact station. For the Trail Center, picnic area and trails, turn right instead.
HOURS	8 AM till dusk
ADMISSION	$4 parking fee weekdays, $5 on weekends & holidays

Handicapped accessible, restrooms, brochures

INTERPRETIVE SITES

Hampton History Museum

120 Old Hampton Lane
Hampton, VA 23669

COUNTY	City of Hampton
PHONE	(757) 727-1610
WEBSITE	*www.hampton.va.us/history_museum*
CONTACT	Michael Cobbs, Curator

TYPE OF HERITAGE SITE
Museum/Cultural Center

HISTORICAL SIGNIFICANCE

Useful, interesting exhibits focus on Kecoughtan daily life at contact, featuring original and reproduction artifacts and graphics depicting Powhatan people's average physical size. Artifacts include pottery, a fish weir, axe, and pipe. A new expansion of this exhibit features a partial Native home, or yehakin, incorporated into the walls.

Interpretive panels describe interaction with English, including trade and conflicts. They describe the Starving Time, Bacon's Rebellion, the 1622 attack by Opechancanough, and William Claiborne's rise as a trader. An additional exhibit describes the development of the Indian School at Hampton during the late 1800s and showcases beadwork from several Western tribes.

HISTORICAL ERAS

A	**Pre-Contact**	*10,000 BCE-1607*
B	**Early Contact and Settlement**	*1607-1622*
C	**Conflict, Reservations, and Treaties**	*1622-1699*
D	**Pre-Revolution**	*1700-1776*
E	Revolution	*1776-1785*
F	Indians and the Creation of the U.S.	*1785-1820s*
G	Jackson and Removal	*1820-1840s*
H	**Civil War and After**	*1860-1880*
I	Darwin, Plecker and Eugenics	*1880-1970s*
J	Fight for Recognition	*1980-present*

PHYSICAL DESCRIPTION

Easy access from I-64, free parking, nearby shops and restaurants.

DIRECTIONS From Williamsburg, take Interstate 64 east to exit 267. At bottom of ramp, bear right onto Settler's Landing Road. At the foot of the bridge, continue straight on Settler's Landing Road. Turn right on Old Hampton Lane. The Hampton History Museum will be on your right as you round the bend. Parking garage is on left.

From Norfolk, take Interstate 64 west to exit 267 (second exit after the bridge tunnel). At bottom of ramp, bear left onto Settler's Landing Road. At the foot of the bridge, continue straight on Settler's Landing Road. Turn right on Old Hampton Lane. The Hampton History Museum will be on your right as you round the bend. Parking garage is on left.

HOURS Monday-Saturday 10–5; Sunday 1–5

ADMISSION $5 Adults, $4 Seniors & Children, $3 Groups (10 or more)

Handicapped accessible, restrooms, brochures

Historic Jamestowne Island

APVA/Preservation Virginia
204 W. Franklin Street
Richmond, VA 23220
Site is located on Colonial Parkway at Jamestown

COUNTY   James City
PHONE   (804) 648-1889
WEBSITE   *www.historicjamestowne.org*

TYPE OF HERITAGE SITE
Historic Park/Natural Area

HISTORICAL SIGNIFICANCE

The Jamestowne Archaearium's exhibits focus on the Virginia Company period and reveal a new understanding of the first English settlers, their relationship with the Virginia Indians, their endeavors and struggles, and how they lived, died and shaped their society. Visitors will discover how archaeologists found the fort. Interactive virtual viewers overlooking the site will virtually transport visitors back in time and show them where objects were recovered and what the fort looked like 400 years ago. The Visitors' Center features new interpretive panels that were written and developed by the eight state-recognized Virginia tribes.

HISTORICAL ERAS

A	**Pre-Contact** 10,000 BCE-1607
B	**Early Contact and Settlement** 1607-1622
C	**Conflict, Reservations, and Treaties** 1622-1699
D	Pre-Revolution 1700-1775
E	Revolution 1776-1795
F	Indians and the Creation of the U.S. 1795-1820s
G	Jackson and Removal 1820-1840s
H	Civil War and After 1860-1880
I	Darwin, Plecker and Eugenics 1880-1970s
J	Fight for Recognition 1980-present

PHYSICAL DESCRIPTION

Located on the James River at the actual site of the Jamestowne Fort.

DIRECTIONS   From Interstate 64, take exit 242-A (Route 199) towards Jamestown. Drive approximately 3 miles to the second traffic light. Turn right at South Henry Street for access to the Colonial Parkway. Take the Parkway towards Jamestown (approximately 7 miles). The Colonial Parkway leads directly to the National Park Service Entrance Station at Historic Jamestowne.

From Surry and the Southside of the James: Take the relaxing 25-minute ferry ride (no charge) from Scotland Wharf to Route 31. Less than a mile from the dock, turn right onto Route 359. The Colonial Parkway is straight ahead, approximately 1/4 mile. Turn right at the stop sign onto the Colonial Parkway.

HOURS   Daily 8:30–4:30
ADMISSION $10 Adult, Children 15 and under, Free

Handicapped accessible, restrooms, brochures

INTERPRETIVE SITES

Jamestown Settlement

Jamestown-Yorktown Foundation
P.O. Box 1607
Williamsburg, Virginia 23187-1607

COUNTY	James City
PHONE	(757) 253-4838; Toll-free (888) 593-4682
WEBSITE	*www.historyisfun.org*

TYPE OF HERITAGE SITE
Museum/Cultural Center

HISTORICAL ERAS

A	**Pre-Contact**	*10,000 BCE-1607*
B	**Early Contact and Settlement**	*1607-1622*
C	**Conflict, Reservations, and Treaties**	*1622-1699*
D	Pre-Revolution	*1700-1776*
E	Revolution	*1776-1785*
F	Indians and the Creation of the U.S.	*1785-1820s*
G	Jackson and Removal	*1820-1840s*
H	Civil War and After	*1860-1880*
I	Darwin, Plecker and Eugenics	*1880-1970s*
J	Fight for Recognition	*1980-present*

HISTORICAL SIGNIFICANCE

At Jamestown Settlement, the stories of the people who founded Jamestown and of the Virginia Indians they encountered are told through film, gallery exhibits and living history. New gallery exhibits and a new introductory film trace Jamestown's beginnings in England and the first century of the Virginia colony and describe the cultures of the Powhatan Indians, Europeans and Africans who converged in 1600s Virginia. Outdoors, visitors can explore re-creations of the colonists' fort and a Powhatan community and also tour a riverfront discovery area to learn about European, Powhatan and African economic activities associated with water. In the outdoor areas, costumed historical interpreters describe and demonstrate daily life in the early 17th century.

PHYSICAL DESCRIPTION

Located on Rt. 31 South, adjacent to Historic Jamestowne, just 10 minutes from the restored area of Williamsburg.

DIRECTIONS From Richmond, take I-64 to Exit 234 (Lightfoot). Turn right onto Route 199. Follow Route 199 for eight miles and turn right at the second traffic light onto Jamestown Road (Route 31).

From Hampton Roads, take I-64 west to Exit 242A. Follow Route 199 for five miles. Turn left at the fourth traffic light onto Jamestown Road.

All: Drive four miles on Jamestown Road, and turn left at the Jamestown Settlement sign, onto Route 359. Turn right into the museum parking lot. Parking is free at Jamestown Settlement.

HOURS Daily 9–5

ADMISSION $13.50 Adults, $6.25 Children

Handicapped accessible, restrooms, brochures, interpretive film, guided tours

Mariners' Museum

100 Museum Dr.
Newport News, VA 23606

COUNTY	City of Newport News
PHONE	(757) 596-2222
EMAIL	*marketing@mariner.org*
WEBSITE	*www.mariner.org*
CONTACT	Kathy Williamson

TYPE OF HERITAGE SITE
Museum/Cultural Center

HISTORICAL ERAS

A	**Pre-Contact** *10,000 BCE-1607*
B	**Early Contact and Settlement** *1607-1622*
C	Conflict, Reservations, and Treaties *1622-1650*
D	Pre-Revolution *1650-1774*
E	Revolution *1775-1790*
F	Indians and the Creation of the U.S. *1790-1820s*
G	Jackson and Removal *1820-1840s*
H	Civil War and After *1860-1880*
I	Darwin, Plecker and Eugenics *1880-1920s*
J	Fight for Recognition *1980-present*

HISTORICAL SIGNIFICANCE

This museum focuses on man's interaction with the sea. It features a small exhibit describing Powhatan boating and fishing activities prior to and during contact with the English. A 17th-century dugout remnant is displayed, along with bone fish hooks and other implements. Recent programs have featured Virginia Indian leaders as speakers, and the museum has republished De Brye's book based on John White's drawings of Native peoples in the area during the late 1500s. They have an original of the book in their collections.

PHYSICAL DESCRIPTION

Easy access from Newport News downtown area.

DIRECTIONS From points North, take I-95 South. Take I-295 Bypass around Richmond. Take I-64 East toward Williamsburg. Take exit 258-A. Travel 2.5 miles to the intersection of Warwick Blvd. and J. Clyde Morris Blvd. (Avenue of the Arts). Continue straight through the intersection and take your first left onto Museum Drive. The Museum entrance is directly ahead.

From Virginia Beach: Take I-64 West. Take exit 258-A. Travel 2.5 miles to the intersection of Warwick Blvd. and J. Clyde Morris Blvd. (Avenue of the Arts). Continue straight through the intersection and turn left onto Museum Drive. The Museum entrance is directly ahead.

HOURS Monday–Saturday 10–5; Sunday 12–5
ADMISSION $12.50 Adults, $7.25 Children ages 6–17

Handicapped accessible, restrooms, brochures, guided tours

INTERPRETIVE SITES

Amazement Square

Fairfax County Park Authority
27 Ninth Street
Lynchburg, VA 24504

COUNTY	City of Lynchburg
PHONE	(434) 845-1888
EMAIL	*visitus@amazementsquare.org*
WEBSITE	*www.amazementsquare.org*
CONTACT	Shawne Farmer

TYPE OF HERITAGE SITE
Museum /Cultural Center

HISTORICAL ERAS

A	**Pre-Contact**	*10,000 BCE-1607*
B	**Early Contact and Settlement**	*1607-1622*
C	Conflict, Reservations, and Treaties	*1622-1689*
D	Pre-Revolution	*1700-1776*
E	Revolution	*1776-1785*
F	Indians and the Creation of the U.S.	*1785-1820s*
G	Jackson and Removal	*1820-1840s*
H	Civil War and After	*1860-1880*
I	**Darwin, Plecker and Eugenics**	*1880-1970s*
J	**Fight for Recognition**	*1980-present*

HISTORICAL SIGNIFICANCE

Amazement Square is a children's museum that takes a novel approach toward education, to engage learning through fun activities. A life-size wigwam has been built into one of the museum's walls. Interior painting illustrates the setting. The paintings continue outside of the replica, illustrating Native life during the Woodland era. As the images progress, modern Monacan people are added to the mural.

Other features include a small dugout canoe, a small hands-on village that children can assemble, and a small display with sand where children can "excavate" and "identify" artifacts. Replicated items such as pottery, stone tools, and bark baskets form one display, and stone artifacts are displayed in a sealed case. An interactive component features interviews with local Monacans discussing history, and powwow footage.

PHYSICAL DESCRIPTION

Adjacent to the James River in Lynchburg, the museum is an old warehouse that has been converted.

DIRECTIONS	On the corner of Jefferson and Ninth Streets along the riverfront in downtown Lynchburg.

HOURS	Tuesday–Saturday 10–5; Sunday 1–5
ADMISSION	General $7, Seniors $6

Handicapped accessible, restrooms, guided tours, brochures

AVOCA

Town of Altavista
1514 Main Street
Altavista, VA 24517

COUNTY   Campbell
PHONE   (434) 369-1076
EMAIL   *avocamuseums@earthlink.net*
WEBSITE   *www.avocamuseum.org*
CONTACT   Frank Murray, Director & Nancy McAndrew,
              Education Coordinator

TYPE OF HERITAGE SITE
Museum /Cultural Center

HISTORICAL ERAS

A	**Pre-Contact** *10,000 BCE-1607*	
B	**Early Contact and Settlement** *1607-1622*	
C	Conflict, Reservations, and Treaties *1622-1699*	
D	Pre-Revolution *1700-1776*	
E	Revolution *1776-1785*	
F	**Indians and the Creation of the U.S.** *1785-1820s*	
G	Jackson and Removal *1820-1840s*	
H	Civil War and After *1860-1880*	
I	Darwin, Plecker and Eugenics *1880-1970s*	
J	Fight for Recognition *1980-present*	

INTERPRETIVE SITES

HISTORICAL SIGNIFICANCE

AVOCA has a small Native American exhibit on the main house second floor. Items were surface-collected in local plowed fields by a past resident of the house. The exhibit displays items from the Paleolithic, Archaic, and Woodland eras. There is a small hands-on exhibit for adults and children, though primarily focused on children. Programs include "A River of Time: American Indian Life in Virginia" (grades K-9). This program focuses on lifestyles of American Indians living in and near what is now Campbell County before contact with Europeans. Students examine clothing, food, tools, and dwellings of Saponi Indians and discuss the impact of Europeans on their society. Another education program is "Westward Go! with Lewis & Clark" (grades 2-8), which traces the journeys of the Lewis & Clark expedition of 1804 and discusses geography, Indian encounters, bartering, food, and more. Programs are SOL-compliant. AVOCA has also hosted public educational days in the past, featuring Native presenters.

PHYSICAL DESCRIPTION
Ten acres, including the main house, gift shop, estate structures, and an outdoor bateaux exhibit.

DIRECTIONS   Located on Rt. 29 Business in Altavista.

HOURS   Thursday–Saturday, 11–3; Sunday 1:30–04:30
ADMISSION $5 or less, depending on age

Handicapped access is limited to first floor (Native American exhibit is on second floor); restrooms, brochures

Bedford City County Museum

210 East Main Street
Bedford, VA 24523

COUNTY   Bedford
PHONE   (540) 586-4520
EMAIL   *bccm-info@bedfordVAMuseum.org*
WEBSITE   *www.bedfordvamuseum.org*
CONTACT   Doug Cooper, Manager

TYPE OF HERITAGE SITE

Museum /Cultural Center, Historic Society

HISTORICAL ERAS

A	**Pre-Contact** 10,000 BCE-1607
B	**Early Contact and Settlement** 1607-1622
C	**Conflict, Reservations, and Treaties** 1622-1699
D	**Pre-Revolution** 1700-1776
E	**Revolution** 1776-1785
F	**Indians and the Creation of the U.S.** 1785-1820s
G	**Jackson and Removal** 1820-1840s
H	**Civil War and After** 1860-1880
I	**Darwin, Plecker and Eugenics** 1880-1970s
J	**Fight for Recognition** 1980-present

HISTORICAL SIGNIFICANCE

The museum showcases Bedford's history from early Native American life through the Civil War and into the 20ᵗʰ century. It is one of the few sites in the Commonwealth that directly and unabashedly gives visitors the entire picture of the Indian experience, from pre-contact through the Plecker era and today. An excellent timeline offers well-researched information that is accessible and interesting.

PHYSICAL DESCRIPTION

Housed in the only example of Romanesque Revival architecture in Bedford, with stone archways, terra cotta ornamentation, and bay windows.

DIRECTIONS   From Roanoke, travel east on Rt. 460 to the left 460 Business exit hat puts you on Blue Ridge Ave., which turns into West Main St. and then East Main St. The Museum is on the left after the 3rd streetlight, 1.5 miles. Parking is next to the building.

From Lynchburg, travel west on 460 to the 460 Business exit. The Museum is on the right, 1.5 miles after the second stoplight.

HOURS   Monday-Friday 10–5; closed Saturday and Sunday, national and school holidays.

ADMISSION $2 suggested donation per adult

Guided tours available by appointment.
Handicapped accessible, restrooms, brochures

Henricus Historical Park

Henricus Foundation & Chesterfield Co.
251 Henricus Park Road
Chester, VA 23836

COUNTY	Chesterfield
PHONE	(804) 706-1340
EMAIL	*henricus1611@aol.com*
WEBSITE	*www.henricus.org*
CONTACT	Pete McKee, Executive Director

TYPE OF HERITAGE SITE
Historic Park/Natural Area

HISTORICAL ERAS

A Pre-Contact
10,000 BCE-1607

B Early Contact and Settlement
1607-1622

C Conflict, Reservations, and Treaties
1622-1699

D Pre-Revolution
1700-1775

E Revolution
1776-1785

F Indians and the Creation of the U.S.
1785-1820s

G Jackson and Removal
1820-1840s

H Civil War and After
1860-1880

I Darwin, Plecker and Eugenics
1880-1970s

J Fight for Recognition
1980-present

INTERPRETIVE SITES

HISTORICAL SIGNIFICANCE

There is a replicated colonial fort and Indian community at Henricus Park. Recent improvements to the Indian community include a palisade, three longhouses, two work shelters, and a hide-tanning area. There is also a fish net-weaving area, an open cooking area, and a garden. The staff exhibits great care in conveying accurate information and hope to make further improvements. The programming here is excellent.

PHYSICAL DESCRIPTION

Henricus Historical Park is replicated in the approximate location of the original Henricus Fort, Established in 1611 on the James River.

DIRECTIONS From I-95, take exit 61A (Rt. 10 East, toward Hopewell). Turn left at the first stoplight onto Old Stage Road (Rt. 732 North) and follow for 2 miles. At the stop sign, make a right onto Coxendale Road (Rt. 615 East) and follow for 1.5 miles. Turn right on Henricus Park Rd. and follow to the Visitor's Center parking lot..

HOURS Tuesday–Sunday 10–5
ADMISSION $6 Adults, $4 Children

Handicapped accessible, restrooms, brochures, guided tours for school groups

Lynchburg Museum

Lynchburg Museum System
901 Court Street
Lynchburg, VA 24504

COUNTY	City of Lynchburg
PHONE	(434) 455-6226
EMAIL	*rachel.deddens@lynchburgva.org*
WEBSITE	*www.lynchburgmuseum.org*
CONTACT	Rachel Deddens, Educator; Gregory Krueger, Curator

TYPE OF HERITAGE SITE
Museum/Cultural Center

HISTORICAL ERAS

A	**Pre-Contact**	10,000 BCE-1607
B	**Early Contact and Settlement**	1607-1622
C	**Conflict, Reservations, and Treaties**	1622-1699
D	Pre-Revolution	1700-1776
E	Revolution	1776-1785
F	Indians and the Creation of the U.S.	1785-1820s
G	Jackson and Removal	1820-1840s
H	Civil War and After	1860-1890
I	**Darwin, Plecker and Eugenics**	1880-1970s
J	**Fight for Recognition**	1980-present

HISTORICAL SIGNIFICANCE

The Lynchburg Museum shares stories about the people and events that have shaped Central Virginia and exhibits treasures of all kinds, with three floors of exhibits. Within the Museum are five galleries. Three media programs focus on people, historic images, and maps.

The main courtroom gallery features a panel exhibit devoted to the Monacan Indian history of the region. A small, accurate display includes a John Smith map replica as well as historic and contemporary images, including text originally developed by Monacan people. Pre-Contact artifacts are gathered in a case. Educational and school outreach programs are available.

PHYSICAL DESCRIPTION

The Lynchburg Museum at the Old Court House is one of the most visible landmarks in Lynchburg. Built in 1855, it stands at the top of Monument Terrace. It is located in Historic Downtown Lynchburg, five blocks from the James River.

DIRECTIONS   Downtown Lynchburg is accessible from Rt. 29 Business and from Rt. 29 Bypass at Exits 1A and 1B. Signs leading to the Museum are well marked. Court Street connects 12th and 5th Streets, and the Museum is accessible from either direction.

HOURS   Monday–Saturday 10–4; Sunday 12–4

ADMISSION $6 General, $5 Seniors, $3–$5 Children

Handicapped accessible (access is limited on weekends), restrooms, tours by appointment, brochures

Virginia Historical Society

428 North Boulevard
Richmond, Virginia 23220
Mail: P.O. Box 7311, 23221-0311

COUNTY City of Richmond
PHONE (804) 358-4901
WEBSITE *www.vahistorical.org/exhibits*

TYPE OF HERITAGE SITE
Museum/Cultural Center

HISTORICAL ERAS

A Pre-Contact
10,000 BCE-1607

B Early Contact and Settlement
1607-1622

C Conflict, Reservations, and Treaties
1622-1699

D Pre-Revolution
1700-1776

E Revolution
1776-1785

F Indians and the Creation of the U.S.
1785-1820s

G Jackson and Removal
1820-1840s

H Civil War and After
1860-1880

I Darwin, Plecker and Eugenics
1880-1970s

J Fight for Recognition
1980-present

INTERPRETIVE SITES

HISTORICAL SIGNIFICANCE

The Virginia Historical Society offers a long-term exhibit that features Native artifacts as part of the larger story of Virginia history. This exhibit includes a dugout canoe. Rotating short-term exhibits occasionally address Virginia Indian themes.

PHYSICAL DESCRIPTION
In downtown Richmond.

DIRECTIONS Take I-95 South/ I-64 East to Exit 78 (Boulevard). Turn right onto Boulevard (heading south). Proceed on Boulevard, crossing over Broad Street, Grace Street, Monument Avenue, and Patterson Avenue. Turn right onto the next street (Kensington Avenue). The VHS is on your left at the corner of Kensington Avenue and Boulevard. Free parking in the VHS lot behind the building.

HOURS Monday–Saturday 10–5; Sunday 1–5
ADMISSION Free on Sundays. Other days $5 Adults; $4 Seniors, $3 Children

Handicapped accessible, restrooms, brochures

MacCallum More Museum

603 Hudgins Street
Chase City, VA 23924

COUNTY	Mecklenburg
PHONE	(434) 372-0502
EMAIL	*mmmg@meckcom.net*
WEBSITE	*www.mmmg.org*
CONTACT	Brenda Arriaga

TYPE OF HERITAGE SITE
Museum/Cultural Center

HISTORICAL ERAS

A	**Pre-Contact** 10,000 BCE-1607
B	**Early Contact and Settlement** 1607-1622
C	Conflict, Reservations, and Treaties 1622-1693
D	Pre-Revolution 1700-1776
E	Revolution 1776-1785
F	Indians and the Creation of the U.S. 1785-1820s
G	Jackson and Removal 1820-1840s
H	Civil War and After 1860-1880
I	Darwin, Plecker and Eugenics 1880-1970s
J	Fight for Recognition 1980-present

HISTORICAL SIGNIFICANCE

MaCallum More Museum is the legacy of the Hudgins family. The artifact collection was locally collected by Arthur Robertson, a past resident of Chase City. Tools and weapons date from 9500 BC to 1600 AD. A life-size replica of Mr. Robertson's log cabin, where he housed his collection, is part of the educational interpretive program. Robertson's journal is included as part of the exhibit and could provide insight as to where many of the artifacts were found. Most of the collection is from Mecklenburg and Halifax counties. The museum sponsors a Native American Day in the spring and an archaeology day in the fall. Participants from Occaneechee and Haliwa Saponi tribes have been involved. The program is designed to fulfill 5th-grade SOLs.

PHYSICAL DESCRIPTION

Five acres including the main house, gift shop, museum and gardens.

DIRECTIONS From Rt. 15 South, turn onto Rt. 47, Craftons Gate Hwy. Follow for 9.3 miles. Turn left onto Walker St. End at Hudgins St.

HOURS Monday–Friday 10–5; Saturday 10–1

ADMISSION $3.50 or less

Handicapped accessible, restrooms, brochures, guided tours

South Boston-Halifax County Museum of Fine Arts & History

1540 Wilborn Avenue
South Boston, Virginia

COUNTY	Halifax
PHONE	(434) 572-9200
EMAIL	*info@sbhcmuseum.org*
WEBSITE	*www.sbhcmuseum.org*
CONTACT	Beth Redd

TYPE OF HERITAGE SITE
Museum/Cultural Center

HISTORICAL ERAS

A Pre-Contact
10,000 BCE-1607

B Early Contact and Settlement
1607-1622

C Conflict, Reservations, and Treaties
1622-1699

D Pre-Revolution
1700-1776

E Revolution
1776-1785

F Indians and the Creation of the U.S.
1785-1825s

G Jackson and Removal
1820s-1840s

H Civil War and After
1860-1880

I Darwin, Plecker and Eugenics
1880-1920s

J Fight for Recognition
1920-present

INTERPRETIVE SITES

HISTORICAL SIGNIFICANCE

The museum exhibits an extensive collection of Native artifacts known as the Abbyville collection. The objects were excavated by local collectors from 1966 to 1970 from several sites on or near Nelson Island, which is now underwater on the Halifax side of Kerr Reservoir. The collection was donated to the museum by Mr. and Mrs. John H. Wells.

The collection of 17th-century objects includes numerous stone tools as well as bone fish hooks, gorgets, awls, and pottery. They are believed to be of Susque-hannock or similar origin rather than Occaneechi. Both tribes inhabited the area during the early colonial era.

PHYSICAL DESCRIPTION

Opened at this location in 1997, the museum originally had 10,500 sq.ft. of space, with an additional 5000 sq.ft. added in 2001.

DIRECTIONS From Richmond, head south on VA-288 toward I-95; merge onto US-360 west toward Amelia. Proceed about 95 miles; turn right on Hodges St., right on N. Main St., left on Edmunds St., right on Wilborn Ave. From Lynchburg area, follow Rt. 460 and Rt. 501 south into South Boston.

HOURS Wednesday–Saturday 10–4; Sunday 2–4:30

ADMISSION Free, donations accepted.

Handicapped accessible, restrooms, brochures

Virginia Museum of Natural History

21 Starling Avenue
Martinsville, VA

COUNTY   City of Martinsville
PHONE   (276) 634-4141
WEBSITE   *www.vmnh.net*

TYPE OF HERITAGE SITE
Museum/Cultural Center

HISTORICAL ERAS

A **Pre-Contact**
10,000 BCE-1607

B **Early Contact and Settlement**
1607-1622

C **Conflict, Reservations, and Treaties**
1622-1699

D Pre-Revolution
1700-1725

E Revolution
1726-1755

F Indians and the Creation of the U.S.
1756-1820s

G Jackson and Removal
1820-1840s

H Civil War and After
1860-1880

I Darwin, Plecker and Eugenics
1880-1970s

J Fight for Recognition
1980-present

HISTORICAL SIGNIFICANCE

At its new, state-of-the-art facility, the Virginia Museum of Natural History hosts a permanent exhibit, "Uncovering Virginia," which focuses on the archaeological recovery of artifacts at a Salem, Virginia site. This site was occupied by Siouan peoples prior to colonization and 150 years thereafter as well, giving archaeologists unusual opportunities to assess cultural change among Native people of the area.

A variety of educational programs have been featured that focus on American Indians, and current programs are being offered.

PHYSICAL DESCRIPTION
Located in downtown Martinsville.

DIRECTIONS   From Richmond, take Rt. 360 southwest to Danville, then Rt. 58 west to Martinsville. Starling Avenue is the main road once you enter the city.

HOURS   Monday–Saturday 9–5:30; Sunday 12–5:30
ADMISSION $9 Adults, $7 Seniors and Students, $5 Children

Handicapped accessible, restrooms, brochures, guided tours for groups

Museum of Middle Appalachians

The Saltville Foundation
P.O. Box 910; 123 Palmer Avenue
Saltville, VA 24370

COUNTY Smyth
PHONE (276) 496-3633
EMAIL *info@museum-mid-app.org*
WEBSITE *www.museum-mid-app.org*

TYPE OF HERITAGE SITE
Museum/Cultural Center

HISTORICAL ERAS

A **Pre-Contact**
    10,000 BCE–1607

B Early Contact and Settlement
    1607–1622

C Conflict, Reservations, and Treaties
    1622–1699

D Pre-Revolution
    1700–1775

E Revolution
    1775–1785

F Indians and the Creation of the U.S.
    1785–1820

G Jackson and Removal
    1820–1840

H Civil War and After
    1860–1890

I Darwin, Plecker and Eugenics
    1840–1970s

J Fight for Recognition
    1980–present

INTERPRETIVE SITES

HISTORICAL SIGNIFICANCE

The Saltville Valley can date its human occupation back 14,000 years. Prehistoric animals visited the valley, attracted by the extensive salt deposits. They were followed by Paleo-Indian hunters. A Woodland-era community was located at the east end of the Saltville Valley. The Museum has an extensive collection of Woodland-era artifacts, including inscribed shell gorgets, recovered locally by Marion native Pat Bass. Also on display are photographs of pictographs found on Paint Lick Mountain in nearby Tazewell County.

PHYSICAL DESCRIPTION

Located in southwest Virginia, in the Saltville Valley, site of the most major salt works in the South during the Civil War.

DIRECTIONS From I-81, take exit 35 and travel 8 miles north on Rt. 107. Follow the signs to the museum.

HOURS Monday–Saturday 10–4; Sunday 1–4
ADMISSION $3 Adults, $2 Children and Seniors

Handicapped accessible, restrooms, brochures

Museum of the Shenandoah Valley

901 Amherst Street
Winchester, VA 22601

COUNTY	City of Winchester
PHONE	(540) 662-1473 or (888) 556-5799 (toll-free)
EMAIL	info@shenandoahmuseum.org
WEBSITE	www.sbhcmuseum.org

TYPE OF HERITAGE SITE
Museum/Cultural Center

HISTORICAL ERAS

A	Pre-Contact *10,000 BCE-1607*
B	Early Contact and Settlement *1607-1622*
C	Conflict, Reservations, and Treaties *1622-1699*
D	Pre-Revolution *1700-1776*
E	Revolution *1776-1785*
F	Indians and the Creation of the U.S. *1785-1820s*
G	Jackson and Removal *1820-1940s*
H	Civil War and After *1850-1860*
I	Darwin, Plecker and Eugenics *1880-1930s*
J	Fight for Recognition *1980-present*

HISTORICAL SIGNIFICANCE

The history of the Shenandoah Valley is presented in the main gallery, which features an excellent presentation on archaeological study in the region, including a discussion of the Thunderbird site, a replica rock shelter, and panels on the PaleoIndian, Archaic and Woodland periods. Interactive exhibits present primary source material from early European explorers. Another set of panels addresses the French and Indian War and Pontiac's Rebellion. Examples of artifacts are displayed.

PHYSICAL DESCRIPTION

The museum campus includes the Glen Burnie Historic House, six acres of gardens, and the 50,000 sq. ft. museum.

DIRECTIONS	From points north: Take I-81 south to Exit 317. Travel south on Rt. 37 to Rt. 50 (Winchester/Romney exit). Turn left onto Rt. 50/Amherst St. Entrance is one mile on right. From points south: Take I- 81 north to Exit 310. Travel north on Rt. 37 to Rt. 50 (Winchester/Romney exit). Turn right onto Rt. 50/ Amherst St. Entrance is one mile on right. From Washington, D.C.: (about 75 miles.) Take I- 66 west to I- 81 north and follow directions above from points south.
HOURS	Tuesday–Sunday 10–4. The house and gardens are open seasonally March –November; museum is open year-round. Closed Mondays.
ADMISSION	Adult: $12 combination ticket (house, gardens, and museum); $10 for museum and gardens; $8 for house & gardens only; $8 for museum only; $6 for gardens only. Youth (7-18), seniors, and groups of ten or more: $10 combination ticket, $9 for museum and gardens; $6 house & gardens only; $6 for museum only; $5 gardens only. Children six and under, free. Garden Audio Tours: admission plus $2/person.

Handicapped accessible, wheelchairs available; restrooms, brochures

Natural Bridge

Lenny Puglizzi
P.O. Box 57
Natural Bridge, VA 24578

COUNTY | Rockbridge
PHONE | (540) 291-1551
WEBSITE | *www.naturalbridgeva.com*
CONTACT | Dean Ferguson, Director of Interpretive Programs

TYPE OF HERITAGE SITE

Privately owned, for-profit facility

HISTORICAL ERAS

A	**Pre-Contact** *10,000 BCE-1607*
B	**Early Contact and Settlement** *1607-1622*
C	**Conflict, Reservations, and Treaties** *1622-1699*
D	**Pre-Revolution** *1700-1776*
E	Revolution *1776-1783*
F	Indians and the Creation of the U.S. *1785-1820s*
G	Jackson and Removal *1820-1840s*
H	Civil War and After *1860-1880*
I	Darwin, Pueckes and Eugenics *1830-1930s*
J	Fight for Recognition *1930-present*

INTERPRETIVE SITES

HISTORICAL SIGNIFICANCE

The Monacan Village is one of the most accurately reproduced Native post-colonial sites on the East Coast used for public education and tourism. The interpretive program focuses on human use of natural resources and Monacan culture. Locally harvested materials—such as cattails, wood posts, saplings and bark—are gathered using replicated tools for the time period (c. 1700). Monacan Indian tribal members work on site, sharing their history with the public. The interpretive area includes a palisade, three work shelters, a wigwam, an open cooking area, an area for weaving mats, a garden, hide-working area, and a staging area for preparing additional shelters.

PHYSICAL DESCRIPTION

The village site is located 300 yards from Natural Bridge.

DIRECTIONS | Located just off I-81, Natural Bridge is at the intersection of Rts. 130 and 11, well marked with signs.

HOURS | Village is open April 1–November 30, 10–5
ADMISSION | $12 Adults

Handicapped accessible, though village access is difficult; restrooms, brochures, guided tours for school groups

RESOURCES

VIRGINIA INDIAN RESOURCES

Virginia Council on Indians
P.O. Box 1475
Richmond, VA 23218
(804) 225-2084
indians.vipnet.org

United Indians of Virginia
Kenneth F. Adams, Chair
1236 Mount Pleasant Rd.
King William, VA 23086
(804) 769-3378

Mattaponi-Pamunkey-Monacan, Inc.
Job Training and Education Consortium
Anne Richardson, Director
(804) 769-4767
www.mpmjobs.org

**Virginia Indian Tribal
Alliance for Life**
Wayne Adkins, President
8836 Sedburg Dr.
New Kent, VA 23124
(804) 932-4406
www.vitalva.org

Virginia Indian Heritage Program
Virginia Foundation for the Humanities
145 Ednam Drive
Charlottesville, VA 22903
(434) 924-3296
www.virginiafoundation.org / VIHP

Chickahominy Tribal Dancers
Wayne Adkins, Coordinator
8836 Sedburg Dr.
New Kent, VA 23124
(804) 932-4406

**Rappahannock American
Indian Dancers**
Judith Fortune, Coordinator
Box 542
Tappahannock, VA 22560
(804) 769-0260

Nansemond Speakers' Bureau
Nita Smith, Director
Richmond, VA
(804) 232-0246
nansemondnita@earthlink.net

WRITING & THINKING
ABOUT VIRGINIA INDIANS

Adapted from the *VCI Journalists' Guide,* approved by the Virginia Council on Indians, September 19, 2006

In the spirit of mutual benefit for historians, anthropologists, journalists, members of the public, and the Virginia Indian communities, the Virginia Council on Indians offers the following helpful suggestions to writers:

1. Take care when using the phrase American Indian, Native American or Virginia Indian "culture." There were numerous Indian cultures in Virginia, and hundreds in North America. Unless you are referring to only one tribe, this word should be plural.

2. Avoid using plurals of names of nations when referring to their people as a group, as in "The Chickahominies shared a reservation with the Mattaponis in the 17th century." When referring to a tribe as a group by their tribal name, the name should always be singular: "The Monacan were recognized by the Commonwealth of Virginia in 1989."

3. Avoid referring to Indian songs as "chants" and to Indian powwow drums with overly dramatic adjectives such as "throbbing." Use the term "regalia" rather than "costumes" for American Indian clothing worn for powwows or ceremonial events.

4. Use discretion when using the word "village" to describe any historic Indian community. Even the 17th century English usually called our communities "towns", as distinguished from temporary "camps" used in seasonal visits for hunting, fishing, and harvesting oysters or various plants for food, medicine and life functions. Terms like "village" and "hamlet" consistently applied to Native American communities imply that our towns were primitive or quaint.

5. Use caution when describing elements of Native cultures in terms that simplify or marginalize, such as "gardening" for "agriculture," "myths" or "legends" for "history," or "woodlands survival skills" for "science."

6. Avoid referring to the paramount chief Powhatan as "Chief Powhatan" as if he were an ordinary chief, or by his informal name Wahunsunacock, when writing about him as a leader. It is appropriate to refer to him as Powhatan, the name (and name of hometown) that he took when he became paramount chief, before the English came to Virginia. This is what other Indian nations called him. The English terms "king", "emperor" and "ruler" are also inappropriate, as they are imperfect English translations used by the colonists who did not understand the nature of his political organization.

7. Powhatan's tributaries (the tribes that paid tribute to him) are best referred to as a "paramount chiefdom" or by using generic terms such as "the Powhatan tribes", when referring to these tribes at the time of English contact. They did not constitute a "confederacy" or a "nation." They were not sub-tribes, but individual nations that paid tribute to the same paramount chief. The only "Powhatan nation" was the tribe located to the east of Richmond on the James River, where the paramount chief came from originally.

8. Virginia Algonquian cultures (indeed, most North American Indian cultures) were matrilineal. A child's status (i.e., being eligible for leadership) was determined by the mother's status, not by the father. Powhatan's high-status wives were known to the English colonists by name, but the mother of Pocahontas was never identified. Therefore avoid referring to Powhatan's daughter, Pocahontas, as a "princess."

9. Use caution when referring to Pocahontas, her age, and the events of her life. It is important to note that opinions differ on the alleged "rescue" incident at Werowocomoco in 1607. Some think it happened much as Smith described it in his 1624 writings, although he did not mention the incident at all in his earlier writing of his time at Werowocomoco. Others think it never happened, and still others believe the event occurred, but was an "adoption" ritual that was misunderstood by Smith.

10. Avoid misinformation about Virginia Indian history, such as incorrect population estimates, referring to the Virginia Algonquians as "Algonquins", or to the Siouan speaking tribes of the piedmont as "Sioux", misspelling the names of tribes, the misrepresentation of events, and using inappropriate language, such as describing periods of intensified English/Indian conflict as "wars."

11. Avoid using only non-Indian "experts" as sources of information about Virginia Indians, whether historical or contemporary. This often results in errors in both historical and modern information, and in the use of inappropriate words, as shown in some of the examples above.

12. Check the facts and use multiple, reliable sources. The Virginia Council on Indians office can supply background information, suggestions for resource material, and referrals to the appropriate tribal leaders as sources for interviews and quotes. The office can be reached via email at *vci@governor.virginia.gov,* or at (804) 225-2084.

RESOURCES

SUGGESTED READINGS

Blanton, Dennis B. and Julie A. King, editors
2004 **Indian and European Contact in Context: The Mid-Atlantic Region.** University Press of Florida, Gainesville.

Beverley, Robert
1947 **The History and Present State of Virginia**, edited by Louis B. Wright. University of North Carolina press, Chapel Hill. *(Primary source material)*

Cook, Samuel B.
2000 **Monacans and Miners: Native American and Coal Mining Communities in Appalachia.** University of Nebraska Press, Lincoln.

* Egloff, Keith, and Deborah Woodward
2006 **First People: The Early Indians of Virginia.** 2nd ed. University of Virginia Press, Charlottesville.

* Feest, Christian F.
1990 The Powhatan Indians. In **Indians of North America**, Frank W. Porter, III, editor. Chelsea House Publishers, New York & Philadelphia. *(Classic secondary source)*

* Gleach, Frederic W.
1997 **Powhatan's World and Colonial Virginia.** University of Nebraska Press, Lincoln. *(Chapter 1 especially recommended)*

Haile, Edward W.
1995 **Virginia Discovered and Discribed by Captayn John Smith 1608.** Map based on Smith and Zuniga maps. Globe Sales Publications, Champlain, Virginia.

* 1996 **England in America: The Chesapeake Bay from Jamestown to St. Mary's City, 1607-1634.** Towns from Smith and Zuniga maps on modern base map. Dietz Press, Richmond, Virginia.

* 1998 **Jamestown Narratives: Eyewitness Accounts of the Virginia Colony: The First Decade 1607-1617.** RoundHouse, Champlain, Virginia. *(Primary source material)*

Hantman, Jeffrey L.
1990. **"Between Powhatan and Quirank: Reconstructing Monacan Culture and History in the Context of Jamestown." American Anthropologist,** New Series, Vol. 92, No. 3 (Sept.), 676-690.

Hantman, Jeffrey L. and Gary Dunham
1993 The Enlightened Archaeologist. **Archaeology**, May/June.

Harriot, Thomas
1972 **A Brief and True Report of the New Found Land of Virginia: The complete 1590 Theodor de Brye edition.** Dover Publications, Inc, New York. Reprinted by University of Virginia Press, 2007, Latin and English. *(Primary source material)*

Houck, Peter W., M.D.
1984 **Indian Island In Amherst County.** Lynchburg Historical Research Co., Progress Publishing Co., Inc.

Kupperman, Karen O.
    2000 **Indians and English: Facing Off in Early America.** Cornell University Press,
    Ithaca, New York.

Moretti-Langholtz, Danielle
    2002 **In Their Own Words: Voices of Virginia Indians.** Video, American Indian
    Resource Center, College of William and Mary, Williamsburg.

    *2003 **In Their Own Words: Voices of Virginia Indians.** Interactive Multimedia CD,
    American Indian Resource Center. College of William and Mary, Williamsburg.

Potter, Stephen R.
    1993 **Commoners, Tribute, and Chiefs: The Development of Algonquian Culture in
    the Potomac Valley.** University Press of Virginia, Charlottesville.

Rountree, Helen C.
    1989 **The Powhatan Indians of Virginia.** University of Oklahoma Press, Norman.
    (Classic secondary source)

    *1990 **Pocahontas's People: The Powhatan Indians of Virginia Through Four
    Centuries.** University of Oklahoma Press, Norman. *(Classic secondary source)*

    1993 **Powhatan Foreign Relations, 1500-1722.** University Press of Virginia,
    Charlottesville.

    2005 **Pocahontas, Powhatan, Opechancanough**: **Three Indian Lives Changed by
    Jamestown.** University of Virginia Press, Charlottesville

Rountree, Helen C. and E. Randolph Turner, III
    2002 **Before and After Jamestown: Virginia's Powhatans and Their Predecessors.**
    University Press of Florida, Gainesville.

* Townsend, Camilla
    2004 **Pocahontas and the Powhatan Dilemma.** Hill and Wang, New York.

Waugaman, Sandra F. and Danielle Moretti-Langholtz
    2006, second edition. **We're Still Here: Contemporary Virginia Indians Tell Their
    Stories**. Palari Publishing, Richmond.

* Wood, Karenne and Diane Shields
    2000 **The Monacan Indians: Our Story**. Monacan Indian Nation, Madison Heights.

Wood, Peter H., et al., editors
    1990 **Powhatan's Mantle: Indians of the Colonial Southeast.** University of Nebraska
    Press, Lincoln.

RESOURCES

---

* *highly recommended for initial research. Classic secondary sources may be somewhat outdated
but are good starting material. Consult primary sources to read what early English authors said
about Virginia Indians.*

CALENDAR OF
VIRGINIA INDIAN FESTIVALS,
POWWOWS, & PUBLIC EVENTS

For an up-to-date calendar of American Indian public events in Virginia and for information on the two traveling exhibits, "Beyond Jamestown" and "Family Portraits," please visit the Virginia Indian Heritage Program website at **www.virginiaindianprogram.org**. For events other than annual tribal powwows, contact organizers prior to attending to ensure that the event is ongoing.

MAR

Final week, Wednesday to Sunday

Virginia Festival of the Book
Book panels and public discussions featuring Virginia Indian leaders and American Indian topics, **Charlottesville**, (434) 924-3296
www.virginiafoundation.org

APR

Final Saturday

Celebration of Life for All People Powwow
Sponsored by Virginia Beach Parks & Recreation. Red Wing Park, off General Booth Blvd., **Virginia Beach**, 11 AM–6 PM (757) 427-2990

MAY

1st weekend

Virginia Indian Nations Powwow & Gathering
Dancing, drumming, crafts, arts, foods. Sponsored by six tribes of Virginia, to benefit our efforts toward federal recognition. Chickahominy Tribal Grounds, Lott Cary Rd., **Charles City**. Sat. & Sun. 10 AM–6 PM. Contact Keith Wynn, (804) 966-2448 • *www.vitalva.org*

3rd weekend, Friday to Sunday

Monacan Annual Powwow
Dancing, drumming, crafts, arts, foods.
Held in Elon, **Amherst County**. Rt. 130, 6 miles west of Rt. 29. Sat. 10 AM–9 PM, Sun. 10 AM–6 PM. Call tribal office (434) 946-0389, or Chief Kenneth Branham (434) 929-7571

4th weekend, Friday to Sunday

Upper Mattaponi Powwow
Dancing, drumming, arts, foods. Tribal Grounds, Sharon Indian School area, Rt. 30, **King William County**. (804) 769-3854

JUN

1st weekend

American Indian Festival
Dancing, drumming, crafts, foods. Co-sponsored by Nansemond Tribe and Chesapeake City Park, Greenbriar Pkwy., **Chesapeake**. (757) 483-6213

3rd Saturday

Mattaponi Powwow
Family event with Indian dancing, drumming, food, crafts. Rt. 30, follow signs to Mattaponi Reservation near West Point, **King William County**. (804) 769-4447

AUG 3rd weekend

Nansemond Indian Tribal Festival & Powwow
A family event sponsored by the Nansemond Tribe, featuring dancing, drumming, and crafts. Lone Star Lakes Lodge, Chuckatuck area, **Suffolk**. Located off Rt. 10 at Pembroke Lane. (757) 986-3354

SEP 1st Saturday

Virginia Indian Day
Family fun on the Potomac riverfront, featuring the Rappahannock Dancers, tribal arts & crafts. Riverbend Park, Great Falls area, **McLean**. (703) 324-8702

4th weekend

Chickahominy Annual Powwow
Dancing, food, crafts. Oldest continuous annual powwow in Virginia, since 1953. Tribal Grounds, Lott Cary Rd., **Charles City County**. Sat. & Sun. 10 AM–6 PM. (804) 966-2448

OCT 1st Saturday

Monacan Indian Annual Homecoming and Bazaar
Family fun, baked goods for sale, scholarship auction, buffet feast. At the Tribal Grounds on Kenmore Rd., **Amherst County**. 10 AM–4 PM. (434) 929-1792 or (434) 929-7571

2nd Saturday

Rappahannock Annual Tribal Powwow
Rappahannock Tribal Center, Rt. 623, Indian Neck Rd., **King & Queen County**. Rt. 360 E to left at St. Stephens Church, follow signs. (804) 769-0260

NOV Wednesday before Thanksgiving

Annual Tribute to the Governor
The Pamunkey and Mattaponi Tribes present tribute of deer and other game to the Virginia Governor as specified by the Treaty of 1646. Governor's Mansion, **Richmond**, 10 AM. (804) 769-2194

DEC TBD

Annual Holiday Dinner
A friendly gathering, with a spectacular buffet. Virginia Indians Tribal Alliance for Life (VITAL), Chickahominy Tribal Grounds, **Charles City County**. Contact Wayne Adkins, (804) 932-4406

Virginia *is for Lovers*

For additional travel and tour information about Virginia, call **800-VISITVA** or see *www.virginia.org*

PHOTOS

Front cover: Sierra Adkins (Chickahominy). Photos by Robert Llewellyn, © 2006.

p. 1: Photo by Robert Llewellyn.

p. 4: Nanny and Paul Miles. Paul was the Pamunkey Chief from 1933-1937. Photo by Samuel Miles.

p. 7: A Sappony elder instructs a younger tribal member in quilting, a traditional activity among many tribes.

p. 8: Footprint of a house pattern, ca. 1600, uncovered by archaeologist in Virginia Beach. Photo courtesy of Keith Egloff, Virginia Department of Historic Resources.

p. 9: Clovis point, ca. 9000 B.C. Photo courtesy of Keith Egloff, Virginia Department of Historic Resources.

p. 10: Mortar and pestle for grinding and preparing food, ca. 3000 B.C. Photo courtesy of Keith Egloff, Virginia Department of Historic Resources.

p. 11: Van Holmes, Chickahominy potter, 1979.

p. 13: Powhatan Red Cloud-Owen (Mohawk/ Chickahominy). Photo by Mathias Tornqvist, 2007.

p. 15: Jerry Fortune (Rappahannock), portraying Chief Powhatan. Photo by Robert Llewellyn.

p. 17: Pontiac Cook (seated) and Andrew Collins, both of the Pamunkey Tribe.

p. 18: Left: Monacan schoolchildren. From the Jackson Davis collection, circa 1914, © 2006 by the Rectors and Visitors, University of Virginia, Special Collections MSS 3072. Right: Parkey Major (Mattaponi), West Point, Virginia, circa 1900. Smithsonian Institution.

p. 19: West shore of Chesapeake Bay. Photo by Robert Llewellyn.

p. 21: Decorating a traditional pot, late 1970s, Chickahominy tribal grounds.

p. 23: Carilyn Sue Branham Elliott (Monacan), with her beadwork, at the Monacan Tribal Center. Photo by Karenne Wood.

p. 25: [Background]: Town of Pomeioc, Theodore DeBry engraving, 1590. [Inset]: Zelma Wynn and Van Holmes (Chickahominy) making pottery, 1979.

p. 27: Photo by Robert Llewellyn.

p. 28: Amy Branham (Monacan). Photo by Mathias Tornqvist.

p. 30: Classic wood-fired urn by Zelma "Deer in Water" Wynn (Chickahominy). From the collection of Karenne Wood. Photo by Mathias Tornqvist.

p. 32: Classic wood-fired pot by Roberta Manakin Adkins (Eastern Chickahominy). From the collection of Gene and Arnette Adkins. Photo by Mathias Tornqvist.

pp. 34-35: Classic blackware by Christine Custalow (Mattaponi). From the collection of Mark Custalow. Photo by Mathias Tornqvist.

pp. 36-37: Traditional honeysuckle baskets by Bertie Branham (Monacan). From the Monacan Ancestral Museum collection. Photo by Mathias Tornqvist.

pp. 38-39: Pre-colonial Powhatan-style structures, created in consultation with Lee Lockamy (Nansemond). First Landing State Park, Virginia Beach, 2006.

p. 40: Terra cotta plate by Kevin Brown (Pamunkey). Blackware vase by Joyce "Pale Moon" Krigsvold (Pamunkey). Terra cotta bowl by Mary A. Bradby (Pamunkey). From the collection of Kevin Brown. Photo by Mathias Tornqvist.

pp. 42-43: Classic wood-fired turtle container with lid, by Voncie "Bright Eyes" Fortune (Rappahannock). From the collection of the Rappahannock Tribal Museum. Photo by Mathias Tornqvist.

p. 44: Classic bowl and spoon by Elizabeth "Blue Water" Adams (Upper Mattaponi). From the collection of Jack and Arlene Milner. Photo by Mathias Tornqvist.

p. 48: Jessica Canaday (Chickahominy) (left), Winona Gear (Monacan) (foreground), at Virginia Indian Nations powwow, 2006. Photo by Robert Llewellyn.

p. 54: Photo by Robert Llewellyn.

p. 78: Clockwise, from top left:

> Molly Holmes Adams (Upper Mattaponi). Photo by Frank Speck, 1926.

> Arlene Milner (Upper Mattaponi), Tribal Council member. Photo by Mathias Tornqvist.

> Ken Custalow (Mattaponi), wood carver and flute maker. Photo by Karenne Wood.

> Karenne Wood (Monacan) with one of four Grandfather Rocks that now grace the site of the National Museum of the American Indian in Washington, D.C. Photo by Jim Pepper Henry, 2003.

> Vanessa Adkins (Chickahominy).

> Two Sappony quilts.

p. 87: Asst. Chief George Whitewolf (Monacan), leather craftsman. Photo by Karenne Wood.